Ethel Winter
and her choreography
En Dolor

Ethel Winter

and her choreography

En Dolor

Edited by Karin Hermes

Text and Score (Labanotation)

Cover photo: Ethel Winter in En Dolor (early costume), 1961
Photography by Jim A. Langley, Courtesy of the photographer
Cover design by Jochen Hermes

Contact and information
karin.hermes@atempo.ch
www.atempo.ch

The musical score and annotated video are available at the

Dance Notation Bureau
151 West 30th Street
Suite 202
New York, NY 10001
212 564-0985 (phone)
212 216-9027 (fax)
dnbinfo@dancenotation.org
http://dancenotation.org

published by
atempo | research & publications
www.atempo.ch

ISBN 978-3-8334-6327-3

Dedication

To all young dancers whose spirit is renewed through movement,
and to all husbands who put up with their crazy schedules.

Ethel Winter

Acknowledgements

The publication of this book would not have been possible without the helpful and unselfish support of many people. Most sincere acknowledgements to all of them for giving their time and professional experience.

Many thanks to Annemarie Parekh for inviting Ethel Winter as one of the outstanding guest teachers at AKAR Modern Dance Studio in Bern, Switzerland. Annemarie is serving the art of dance with all her energy and her inspiring, demanding and sustaining support. Without Annemarie this book would also not have been possible.

Without Charlie Hyman this book would not have developed as it is. Many thanks to him for making collected material of Ethel's career available.

Many thanks to Noelle Simonet and Jean Jarrel for investing much time on two practical score checkings. Jean's corrections of the whole manuscript as well as her thoughtful advice concerning the structure of this book were helpful and encouraging.

Ann Hutchinson-Guest and Jacqueline Challet-Haas to be acknowledged for their most precious corrections on the score.

Kathryn Eggert spend much time collecting data which hopefully provide useful material for dance researchers. She also provided material for Victoria Geduld to write the chapter "Ethel Winter – Dancer, Choreographer, Teacher". Many thanks to them both.

For the lay out, technical support and the final publishing process Jochen Hermes is gratefully appreciated. And finally David Hyman to be acknowledged for his transfer of information.

Table of Contents

Introduction

I believe dancers need more than perfect technique. They need to perfect using it. That's why when Karin Hermes suggested working on this notation project I was excited. Here was an opportunity to provide a vehicle for students to practice performance skills. Musicians have their etudes to study and play so why shouldn't dancers have the same advantage. Karin is one of our most brilliant notators so I felt safe in her hands. To quote Muriel Topaz, she said to me "Karin is a genius at notation." It was a great privilege to work with her and learn more about the perfection of detail through notation.

I hope this enterprise will prove helpful to the dancer who wishes to enter the performance arena. My sincere gratitude and thanks to those who have contributed their time and energies. To Karin for her caring and dedication; to Kathryn for her making sense out of collected chaos; to Victoria for putting it altogether; to Charles for saving printed materials I thought had been thrown out.

Ethel Winter
New York City, 2006

Foreword by Annemarie Parekh

Ethel Winter has been my teacher ever since the 1960s, when I studied dance in New York. Years later, she taught summer courses at my Akar Modern Dance Studio in Bern, Switzerland.

In 1997 Karin Hermes and I met in Paris. She was recreating a choreography for a junior company, and I was guest teaching. We liked working together, so she came to Bern to set pieces on my student group.

When Ethel offered to teach her "En Dolor" to my repertory class in 1999, Karin decided to learn this solo, too. She was deeply impressed by Ethel's mastery in teaching and choreographing, and out of appreciation she proposed to notate "En Dolor". This is how the long and fascinating process started that lead to this publication.

Learning to perform "En Dolor" was an experience that gave our students a new understanding of the art of dance, its depth and timelessness. Seeing Karin learn, perform and notate the choreography opened their eyes for the meaning and need of notation.

Observing and accompanying the process of teaching, notating and collecting data for this publication gave me new insights. It also evoked memories and a deep feeling of love and gratitude for all the guidance I had received from Ethel as a teacher, coach and friend. And it made me appreciate and admire Karin's talents, her dedication and persistence without which this work could not have been completed.

Annemarie Parekh
Bern, 2006

Foreword by Karin Hermes

I first became acquainted with Ethel Winter in July of 1999 at Akar Modern Dance Studio in Bern, Switzerland, where she was teaching a summer course in Graham Technique and repertory. As a participant of the workshop I was deeply impressed with Ethel Winter as a master teacher. The workshop participants were from many different technical levels and backgrounds yet in spite of this, there was a unity in the class. With clarity and sensitivity, she skillfully brought these differences together into a cohesive working environment.

Beyond her technical mastery and wonderful sense of musicality, Ethel is a positive and uplifting teacher. With her incredibly experienced background she is able to reach students very quickly. She has something to say about the meaning of dance and shares it with students. "Dance is communication" she says in class. "Dance needs patience" is another phrase which stayed with me for a long time.

Ethel Winter is a dedicated artist and teacher who transmits a living vision of dance both in the major international projects she undertakes as well as in the small things and all with an impressive modesty. She has so much to give and hence my desire to include with the notated Solo of "En Dolor" a publication about Ethel Winter.

Karin Hermes
Bern, 2006

ETHEL WINTER

Ethel Winter, 1957
Photography by Charles Hyman
Courtesy of the photographer

A Conversation with Ethel Winter

The interview was conducted by Kathryn Eggert and Karin Hermes during Ethel Winter's guest teaching residency at Akar Modern Dance Studio in Bern, Switzerland, in April 2000 and April 2001.

As a dance student at Bennington, who were your most influential teachers at that time?

Martha Hill was a big influence for me. She started the dance department at Bennington College and later also started the department at the Juilliard School.

Being open and very forward looking, she was responsible for most of the exchange programs where professional artists came to Universities to teach and perform. Without laying this foundation the companies of Graham, Humphrey-Weidman, Hanya Holm and others would not have had the opportunities for residencies, which allowed them to bring their professional work to students studying the craft. The other big influence was William Bales. He was our main technical teacher and had been with the Humphrey-Weidman Company. His wonderful energetic spirit infused us all. Especially after staying up all night writing a paper, his enthusiasm helped chase away fatigue!

You once said, "as a dancer I love; much like an actress finds her character in the written word, to make movement phrases speak." Did you have much of a theater acting background during your studies?

Yes, I did have some basic acting courses at Bennington and many of the technical things you had to do became very handy to me as a dancer. When I was acting, I had a lot of trouble with improvisation if it was the spoken word. However, if we were suppose to do a character with a physical affect or disability, I was very good. The whole process is much the same really. I always found it necessary to find out "who I was" in order to do the movement the way it should be done to communicate what was intended.

Why do you think Martha Graham chose you to be the first dancer to take over her roles?

When I was first taken into the Graham Company, I took over many different roles. I first danced the roles of Sophie Maslow, Nina Fonaroff and Pearl Lang, so Martha knew I had a range. When I took over Martha's roles, I never tried to be Martha. I couldn't be more different. I am not sure exactly why she chose me but I hope it was because she could see that I had a large and varied movement range. On the other hand I think Martha just thought that one would either sink or swim. She had that about her.

Are there any differences in your approach when you are learning a dramatic role versus a dance role without such a defined character?

Well there are some slight differences yet even with a dance role you still have to find something that defines your dancing and allows clarity of intention in your movement. I still want to know "Who I am" in a piece whether it has a strong defined character or not. With a character role it is easier to know who you are and you can work from this. For example, Diversions of Angels doesn't have a dramatic story but depends on qualities and images. In doing "The girl in Red", I used the unpredictable nature of a fire and its' flames. One could be slow burning or fast burning. In Seraphic Dialogue, the character of St. Joanne is used to show personal struggle. Since Joanne acted on faith it seemed very right to use the word commitment as motivation. This one word influenced very much how I performed the role.

As a dancer, is it easier to have a new role created on you?

Yes, as you are a part of the process. The choreographer gives to the dancer and the dancer feeds back to the choreographer. Martha would define the character for you and since you knew the movement vocabulary, you could change the coloration and quality of the movement to fit the character. When she would create a role, she would often tell you who you were, what the section was and the qualities she wanted but not give you any so called steps. Upon leaving the room she might say, " Would you play with this part of the music awhile? " There are some dancers who say "Oh I choreographed my part." Well, it is not totally true! The sense of the structure and everything that goes into it belongs to Martha. The steps are in a way secondary. Martha had great vision in the way that she used people. It's like an artist making a woodcarving or sculpture. He must have the ability to choose the right material.

14

When Martha began to pass on her roles, did she teach them step by step?

No. She did that more in the later years than she did earlier. She would work mainly from the dramatic, which is very important. The steps don't mean that much really. However, Martha did have certain idiosyncrasies. In Frontier for example, it must be the left leg that is on the fence very high and turned in because her left leg was terrific in extension. Unfortunately for me, when I took over the role, my right leg was the terrific one in extension! Eventually, it takes a toll on your body and I am sure that's why I had to have my left hip replaced. The most important thing was to know what the meaning of the dance. Martha would spend some time, but not very much. That's why I say a little of it was the challenge, "are you going to make it or not". On the other hand you could say, "well, maybe she trusts me."

Martha Graham talked in an interview about her desire to "reveal the interior landscape." What does this statement mean to you?

Martha would also say this in another way, "The temperature chart of the heart" or the "beat of the heart" reveals the innermost feelings of the character. Martha was never interested in purely decorative dance or simple storytelling. Her aim has always been for a fusion of form and content and to use this to unveil human psychology in her work. She always wanted to know why. She believed dance had a great ability to expose the human heart and mind.

Once you said in an article, "When you are performing a role, you learn about the role. You are probably learning for the first time what you really are going to do with that part when you are out on stage. It takes a while to grow in a role." Can you give an example of this?

Yes, this really happened for me with the role in Herodiade. It was very revealing to me on stage during the first performance. I can't really say why or what happened, only that something did happen. It is a strange piece because it is about the creator and about death. When something is being created there is also another part which is dying. Within creation the cycle goes on, from death there comes creation. When you are totally into the role, certain things really become revealed to you. When you are so into the role you don't even think about technical things at all. What makes the magic in a performance, is how you are connecting with the audience and how they are connecting with you. When that is missing, it is not good because you won't perform well.

I remember when I first had to dance the role of "the Girl in Red" in Diversion of Angels, I was very nervous. She has a difficult entrance and must enter the stage in a tilt and stay there before she continues across the stage. I had to find something for that moment because otherwise you just keep saying I have to keep my balance! Then I remembered I once read something that Ruth St. Denis said and it really helped me. She said that she kept very quiet before a performance because she knew she had to give to the audience in a way to make them fall in love with you. I found this to be true and very helpful. You give so completely as a performer.

You have traveled so many places around the world as a performer and choreographer. Do you have any tours you found especially memorable and what impressed you most during your travels as a performer?

My first tour with the Graham Company was memorable because it was not easy. We were touring across the states in 1946 and this was just after the war. We went by train and they were not in good shape. Good food was not available at this time because of the rationing. All in all it was an exhausting adventure although the audiences received us well. Later on in 1954, the Asian tour was wonderful. The Asian people welcomed us genuinely. They loved Martha Graham's work because they could relate so well to her myths and stories. I remember that in Sri Lanka, they especially loved A Seraphic Dialogue because of the costumes. We wore these bright colorful robes of red, green and blue and the people loved it. I guess it is the landscape they know and the home of colorful birds! Israel was at the end of the Asian trip and it was also exciting. We felt like we returned to civilization a little bit as we could get some simple food like tomatoes and cheese.

Regarding your own choreographic work, what influenced your own creative work?

The arts, poetry, literature and music.

Did you eventually feel the need to break away from the Graham vocabulary?

I was always known as a lyrical dancer. It's just that I don't always hit the movement. That's why I enjoyed working with Sophie

16

Maslow. Even though she came out of Graham, she had another take on it. To me, that is what is quite amazing about what Graham did for dance. When I think of Anna Sokolow, Merce Cunningham and Sophie Maslow coming from this background yet all going into a different direction, I think that says something about what a great force Graham was.

Did you give the dancers in your company defined roles and movements or were they involved in the creation of their roles as well?

With my company I had to be more specific with the given material. My dancers were mainly dance students from the Graham school and I had to take them and create a unit. Once you finally got them there with the movements, someone would leave for a bigger Company. It was hard to keep the same dancers together and I spent a lot of time resetting the roles, which left little time to do new ballets.

What qualities were you looking for in dancers for your company?

Of course I wanted people who looked good on stage and who had good technique but it wasn't the only and most important thing. It was just as important that they had a personality and had something to say as a performer.

Which of your own works have you set on other students or companies?

En Dolor, Spiritual Passages, Fun and Fancy and Suite of Three

Many of your works had original music composed for them. How did you go about choosing your composers?

I had already developed a working relationship with many of them. For instance, Eugene Lester was at first, Martha Graham's pianist and rehearsal director and later became the conductor. So I knew him very well and it was easy to work with him. At first I would come in and show him some of the choreography and then he would play something. When I was teaching at Bennington, Joseph Liebling was there as the musical director and composer for dance so I knew what his music would be like. Gwen Watson had accompanied me out on the West Coast and then she came to the East Coast. So I had a rapport with all of the composers I used.

I would like to talk about the preservation of dance. The repertoire of Graham is very limited to access. The Graham Company performs the work but very few other companies are allowed to do it. Do you think it is possible to

*capture the inner meaning of Graham's choreography if one didn't dance
with her personally or with the company?*

I once saw American Ballet Theatre doing Diversion of Angels and
they are all beautiful dancers, but they where not given enough
time. If you rehearse in your own style you can get something
quickly. But when it is something else, it takes a while. It wasn't
terrible, but after all, it is going to be slightly different. The men
were wonderful at jumping, but they were dancing with a very
"light" quality, which is very different from what the "Graham men"
are. That's all right. I mean I've seen Hamlet done very many times
in different ways too. But unfortunately for the dancers, they were
physically hurting themselves because they didn't have time to
think and therefore dance differently.

Does it make sense to go on with the Graham work?

Oh, I think it makes sense because we are training our dancers for
all kinds of experiences. For example the Juilliard students all have
to spend equal time training in the various techniques. We are training them to be able to have a broader range because many modern
choreographers are working with ballet now.

*It is known that Martha Graham kicked dance notators out of her studio.
Was she afraid to have them misinterpret the work and that the inner
meaning of the work would be lost?*

Yes, she was afraid that it would not be done correctly. Martha used
to say that when she died she wanted it all to die with her.

For example Muriel Topaz notated Diversions of Angels, many
years ago, but she had to promise to put the score in a vault. I can't
remember under what circumstances it can be brought out, but
anyway it's there. I know another woman who started to notate
Dark Meadow but then somehow she had to stop. Possible they had
run out of funds because it is very expensive to do. I feel it was a
great shame. I think if you have got a notated score and a good
video it is possible to preserve a piece. There are some videos in
existence but very often we don't bother to correct them and we
should! Sometimes something isn't done correctly or the space isn't
right and those things should be corrected.

I can remember Ann Hutchinson coming to see us in the 40's and
wanting to notate a work but Martha wouldn't hear of it. Well, there

18

were certain things she was very conservative about and she just didn't believe in it. But she didn't understand it either; she didn't take the time to know what was really possible. We all know that it depends on who plays the Bach piece how it comes out. Back in the 40's good dancers were not as available or well trained as they are today so she did have legitimate suspicions. I think notation is very valuable and I am sorry that Martha had the feeling that she didn't want anything to live after her.

Do you think a dancer of today is faced with different challenges than a generation ago as far as working and trying to maintain a healthy balance in their life and career?

Yes, there are a lot of differences. For one thing, I never thought of dance particularly as a source of living. But many of today's dancers do. That's okay, there are many more options today for dancers to get work, like TV and MTV, if they need to earn money and are looking for security. But actually a dancer doesn't really have that much security and they are always subject to injury. That's why Martha had a School where we could teach and earn a living. But the way I always felt was if you love something, the money and the security were secondary to having a passion for one's work.

Can you compare the situation in Europe and America? Is there a different approach you take in your teaching?

Actually I like people to be able to relax in class. I find if people are afraid of you, or if they think "I must do this or I will be kicked out", it becomes a negative working experience. You have to let them feel that they should do it to the best of their ability. It is different if you are working with different levels of course, but is doesn't mean my attitude isn't the same in terms of wanting them to do the best they can.

Do you think the Graham technique is better understood by dancers from an American cultural background versus dancers from various cultural backgrounds?

There is a difference. It's true. The urgency of the technique and the directness is sometimes missed. I taught in Hawaii and since the weather is nice and the palm trees sway in the breeze, it was hard to get that urgency. Even here in Switzerland, people are very polite. I never feel that anyone would confront me here, or ask me - "why I do something a certain way" – and I am perfectly willing that they would ask just to get a little dander up. And that's all the more reason that I want them to feel relaxed in class so that they will ask a question, because that's when they get involved, when they ask questions.

Is that easier to get from dancers in the United States?

Oh, yes (laugh) oh yes, they ask lots of questions.

In a professional Dance Education program, what do you think is important to pass on to an aspiring dancer besides technique?

I am worried about the fact that we are in a computer age and everybody is doing everything by the numbers. I am worried about the humanity and the spirit. I think dance has that particular quality that can project the spirit. When I see some things that are just athletic and technical, yet beautifully done, it just doesn't grab me. I'd rather see someone working from the heart.

You accomplished so many things in your life. Dancing and touring for a major company, teaching across the States and abroad, starting your own company and having a family. How did you manage to keep it all in balance?

Well first of all, remember that those things were for specific periods of time. If you have a show to perform, then you had to stay there and do it every night no matter what. It is a schedule just like any work schedule, so that part isn't so hard. But I think you have to have a very cooperative husband who understands when you are at a rehearsal until 11:00 at night. Otherwise it doesn't work if they don't understand what goes into the whole thing.

I guess my son thought it was all very normal because he grew up with it. I can remember once when he was very young, about 3 years old, I left him overnight with my inlaws. Well, he kept asking Charlie's mother what she did and she said, " Well I get the meals and….." My son interrupted her and said " No, but what do you do? " In other words he expected her to have another profession. It was just normal for him that his mother had another profession. It wasn't that I was away all the time. He had a lot of quality time.

You have been for nearly a century on the top of the international dance world and have lived through the development of American Modern Dance. Is there anything you would like to share with future dancers?

20

I don't know exactly what to share, but I do find that there are much better dancers around than in my days, technically speaking, as there is better training available now. Whether they are more memorable, like we remember Isadora Duncan, Mary Wigman and others, I'm not sure. But I find that today, in taking up dance as a profession, so much is expected of a dancer that they usually wear out in 15 years. Whereas in my generation, even though we wore out, we danced for a very long time and we stayed on teaching. I know a lot of students from Juilliard who have already gotten out of dance because they were over used. I find that sad. That you dedicate so much of your life and time and spirit but then again … that may be up to each individual.

Affiliate artist speaks

by Miss Ethel Winter, 1967

This lecture was given at Hood College, Maryland

One always tries to think of a clever way to start the remarks. I never can so I shall just be simple. I'm very happy to be here at Hood as an artist affiliate, but it has its amusing side. When I first heard of the program and read its aims, I was struck with the repetition of the one world – articulate. The artist must be articulate. The language of words has never been easy for me. This is precisely why I became a dancer. It's a little ironic to be here now, doing the thing that terrorizes me most – but the possibility of sharing some of the excitement and joy I feel about dance is a challenge I had to accept.

Often the performing artist is looked upon as someone different, even strange, apart from the main scene. I would like to suggest another picture. The performer works for years perfecting his craft and skills in order to give that inspired performance. So too, the scientist works for years perfecting his skill and knowledge, his end being, perhaps, to find an answer to the unknown. The attainment of these skills has much in common.

I am going to borrow from something I read in Eric Fromm's book The Art of Loving. He states that there are four requirements necessary: discipline, concentration, patience and supreme concern. I see these four requirements as pertinent to everyone and to the practice of any art or activity – whether the performing lawyer, dentist, writer, student or teacher. Naturally I would like to discuss these requirements with an eye especially to the preparation of a dancer.

Discipline

A dancer and his instrument are one and the same. The training of this instrument is a constant reality. It takes hundreds and hundreds of pliés to make that one exciting leap. It takes hundreds and hundreds of contractions to make the one that will eventually contain the meaning and communication for which one strives. So the dancer trains. This requires physical work every day – a class or rehearsals. Not just in season, but 52 weeks out of the year would be fine. It requires sensible decisions about rest an play – you just might have to give up a party or two or at least leave early. His training becomes a kind of insurance policy. Each profession has its hazards: the surgeon is concerned with his hands, a cut means he can't operate; the singer, his voice. The dancer multiplies this – a bad ankle, knee, back, shoulder would put him out of commission. If he keeps his instrument tuned with constant work, he cuts down the possibility of serious injury.

Technical skill and physical brilliance gives one great power. But this is only a means to an end – not the end itself. If one wishes to do just the stunt or trick, fine – I love it – but join the circus. I see dance as something much more than this, something that can portray a large range of feelings and emotions – the inner life of the being – those emotional and spiritual experiences present in everyone. Miss Graham has described this as the "interior landscape" or "the temperature chart of the heart".

A disciplined instrument can realize these moments, an undisciplined one will do it only by chance. I mention this because too often contemporary dance is confused with a kind of creative free expression. Yes, we want to make an expressive instrument, but a knowledgeable one. The dancer tries to evoke the emotions of the spectator – very different from emoting. For the dancer, it is always a conscious and calculated action.

This may sound terribly traditional to some of you if you are acquainted with the new experiments and avant-garde movements. But this is what dance is to me and to negate feeling from movement is like negating the fact that one is human.

This summer I was teaching a summer workshop at San Francisco State. The evening before I was to begin teaching, I questioned some of the to-be-students about what was going on in the area. There were many experiments happenings different from New York area, but I did feel I was going to be looked upon as a complete square. So I took the bull by the horns, told them what my beliefs were and proceeded to work them very hard. They loved the discipline and results. Many said they had never worked that way before. My point of this digression is that, if one is going to be a rebel, it seems very important to know what the rebellion is about.

How many of you here think of dancing as a kind of frivolous, gay, carefree activity? A good many, I suspect. It has great ability to express the exuberant an joyous, but one certainly doesn't live in that state. For the serious dancer who wishes to encompass the magical world of theatre, it is a life of self-discipline and dedication.

Concentration

Movement never lies. It tells a great deal about us. The greatest number of injuries occur when we are too tired or emotionally upset. Your concentration is split. The performer very often is working under conditions where there is great emotional stress and fatigue. It is essential for him to do what he is doing when he is doing it.

I remember once after a demonstration class with Miss Graham, a visitor commented – there seems to be something about your work that is religious. Miss Graham's answer was to suggest that perhaps the words whole and holy were not too far apart. For holy means to give one's whole self, in the usual sense, to God or one's beliefs. The dancer too must give his whole self to the instant – a complete coordination of mind, body and spirit.

Last year while I was sitting on a jury board at Juillard for entrance exams in Dance Department, (it is a professional school so we expect a few years of good training), one boy auditioned who had had little formal work. He said, however, "I have had a year of performance diving". Well, I wasn't too impressed with this information, but it proved very enlightening. He performed his dance brilliantly. His total intent on what he was doing made the content show. You see, he knew on the diving board that each and every move could make the difference between success or failure, injury or brilliance. His dance performance carried over the ability to believe, to concentrate, and to know that the instant matters.

Patience

It's hard to have patience when everything around you seems to be moving at jet speed. When people ask how long it takes to become a dancer, they are often surprised with the answer. It takes a good 10 years – plus. And it can't be hurried too much. Sometimes students think if they take 3 technique classes a day, they will become proficient 3 times as fast. It's not so. Like everything else, you have to digest what you're taking in. Intensive work for a short time is fine, but generally the slow and steady wins.

You must have the patience to endure and enjoy repetition – those hundreds and hundreds of pliés I spoke of, those hundreds and hundreds of contractions, beats, triplets, and on and on. You must have the patience for the repetition of caring for the instrument. Every time one performs or rehearses, the body has to be warmed up. You wouldn't start your automobile in high gear because the machinery would break down. Well, so too this instrument.

Supreme Concern

I remember watching a television program which was an intimate visit with Pablo Casals as he was rehearsing. He went over a particular musical phrase time and time again deciding how to coordinate technical difficulties with the desired phrasing and color. It was marvelous to see this great master, and realize that without our first requirements we would never reach this highest point of supreme concern.

So the artist is eventually in complete control of his material and does what he does through choice and knowledge – and because he cares.

The disciplined dancer, and now I mean one committed to these 4 requirements, is usually the inspired one. By inspired, I mean literally to breath into – to breath into means to give something life. Now, there are many well trained performers who never do this. They have learned what to do on the outside but not what to do from the inside – again the involvement of the whole person, the spirit, the soul, the imagination, whatever one wishes to call it. I can lift my arm and I can lift my arm. The first is outer and design – the second is inner and with a commitment to the act. So for me dancing is not just the conventional pretty and graceful but anything one feels compelled to communicate – and in a theatre form there must be communication.

There is one more ingredient – the performer needs you – the audience. This can be magic. The audience can make or destroy a performance. Your participation is essential – the interchange from the

25

performer, that particular projection the audience responds to and then gives back to the performer. It doesn't always happen but when it does – it's magic.

Ethel Winter, rehearsal in studio, 1957
Photography by Charles Hyman
Courtesy of the photographer

Ethel Winter, rehearsal in studio, 1957
Photography by Charles Hyman.
Courtesy of the photographer

Ethel Winter, 1957
Photography by Charles Hyman
Courtesy of the photographer

Ethel Winter: Dancer, Teacher, Choreographer
by Victoria Geduld, 2004-2005

Ethel Winter toured throughout the United States, Europe, and the Orient as a dancer, teacher, and choreographer. For over twenty years, Winter performed with the Martha Graham Dance Company; she was the first dancer to perform roles originated by Miss Graham in Salem Shore, Night Journey, Herodiade, El Penitente, and Frontier. In addition, Winter portrayed Joan of Arc in Seraphic Dialogue, and the Bride in Appalachian Spring. Graham created roles for Winter such as Helen of Troy in the full length ballet, Clytemnestra, Cleopatra in One More Gaudy Night, and Aphrodite in Phaedra. Winter's performances were met with critical acclaim: in Night Journey she was called, "the Jocasta of our time." Winter's versatility was heralded: "Ethel Winter makes Aphrodite permeating vulgar and vicious, although half an hour earlier she was the most beautiful and heartbreaking Joan of Arc." In addition to her work with the Graham Company, Winter worked extensively with Sophie Maslow; she performed on Broadway, for television, and in films. Winter choreographed for her company, The Ethel Winter Dance Company, and has set her works on dance companies throughout the world. Her varied teaching career includes faculty positions at numerous Universities in the United States and many guest positions abroad.

Ethel Winter was born on June 18th, 1924, in Wrentham, Massachusetts, a small town between Boston and Providence, Rhode Island. The youngest of three children, Winter's father had remarried after the death of his first wife. Ethel's mother was the younger sister of his first wife, so Ethel shared paternity with her brother and sister. Winter called her father's remarriage, "very Biblical."

Neither of Winter's parents shared her interest in theatrical dance: Ethel's mother, who taught grade school before marriage, had an interest in music; Her father, an inventor and businessman, was a keen sportsman. Winter says: "I know my mother really loved to dance. We used to do square dancing on Saturday nights in the Town Hall. I know that sounds kind of old fashioned, but it was fun." When Ethel's elder sister began taking dance classes with a neighborhood teacher, she insisted on joining. Although thought too young at the age of five, she persisted. Considered "more talented than the rest," the teacher encouraged her to continue dance training.

Winter's upbringing was steeped in the family's New England Puritanical background. Although dancing was not forbidden, she was only allowed to take extensive classes on Saturday with the promise that she would attend church and Sunday school the following day. Not deterred by her Puritanical upbringing in which the dance was not considered an acceptable profession, Ethel danced and tapped throughout the house "driving her family crazy." She reflects: "My parents were afraid of the theatre. It was seen as an evil influence. And now that I look back on it, dance really wasn't respected that much. Martha Graham really helped make it a respectable theatre experience."

At the age of eleven, Winter saw the opera, The Magic Flute. She says: "I still remember how my skin tingled when the curtain rose!" In 1938 she saw Ballet Russe de Monte Carlo and recalls being thrilled by the dance and the music in Gaite Parisienne with Alexandra Danilova and Leonard Massine. That same year she saw one of the final performances of Ted Shawn and his all male modern troupe. These were her only early experiences seeing theater.

Winter excelled in school as well as in sports. Her father taught her to play many sports. "My father used to take me out, to ice-skate, and play tennis and golf. He seemed to enjoy it. He was very supportive of my athletics in high school, my basketball and all of that. But Art he didn't get at all!" Although she considered pursuing ice-skating professionally, Ethel decided at an early age that she wanted to dance, perhaps due to her love of music.

At the start of high school, Winter convinced her mother to drive her into Boston twice each week for dance lessons at the Lilla Villes Wyman School where she studied ballet, tap, Spanish, classical Indian, and acrobatics: "Anything they offered I wanted to do." At sixteen, Winter drove herself into Boston for classes. She remembers how really shocked an aunt was, who felt Ethel's mother was crazy to foster such freedom. As Ethel grew close to completing high school, she expressed her desire to continue dancing in New York City. During the early 1940s, there were few opportunities for professional dancers in the United States: "In my day there really wasn't that much dance that one could do. I wanted to come to New

York City because the only thing you could possibly think of doing to make a living was to join the Rockettes. There was no ballet company in Boston; there was no ballet company in New York." Winter's parents insisted that she go to college, so she chose Bennington, an excellent liberal arts college for women with a renowned program in dance.

At Bennington, Winter's dance technique quickly expanded beyond her early training. Martha Hill, who established the Bennington Summer Festival and college program, and later established the dance department at the Juilliard School, was a huge influence on her. Hill's professional outlook at Bennington exposed Ethel to a myriad of dance styles. William Bales, a noted performer and choreographer who had been with the Humphrey-Weidman company, was Ethel's primary technique teacher. Winter also took acting classes at Bennington which she said became "very handy" to her as a dancer. "As a dancer, I loved – much like an actress finds her character in the written word – making movement phrases speak."

Bennington opened up the dance world to Ethel, and also allowed the exploration of her own sense of the world that had been developing since childhood. She recalls: "It wasn't until I got to college that I was able to find things that were consistent with how I took on the world. Because I found people very hypocritical. You know, they'd say one thing, and they would act another way. And in a small town you see that very easily. Now here's hypocrisy for you: I loved to play cards. But my mother would never let us play cards in the front room on Sundays where somebody might see us. It had to be in the back room. It was the same thing with tennis. If we went out we had to be sure that there weren't people watching. I just found that kind of amusing." This early intolerance of hypocrisy and injustice stayed with her throughout her life.

Due to the national impact of World War II (WWII), the summer dance festival at Bennington did not take place after Winter's freshman year. However, during the month of June, Graham, Louis Horst, her musical director, and the company were invited to Bennington for a residency. During the company's stay, Graham worked on new pieces. Horst taught choreography to dance majors including Winter. In 1943, Graham created Deaths and Entrances at Bennington which Ethel credits with being one of her early formative theatrical experiences. During the performance, a thunder and lightening storm broke out and accented the dark piece. Winter remembers being enthralled with the "emotionally intriguing" work. In her junior year, the summer of 1943, Winter was asked to join the company and perform in Every Soul is a Circus. She was thrilled to be invited to dance with the company. At the end of the concert, Ethel learned her first lesson from Graham. "Just after the company bow, Miss Graham came out for her solo bow and then proceeded to insist that I join her for a special bow. I resisted because I had only danced a small part and felt that I was not deserving of an extra bow. Miss Graham took the time to explain that this was false modesty. She said: "A performer should realize that a bow is simply a thank you to their audience and one should accept it graciously.""

Due to fuel rationing for the War efforts, Bennington students were required to participate in outside projects and internships during the winter. So in her senior year (winter of 1944), Ethel went to New York to study at the Graham School and learn the repertory. She was selected to go on a six week tour with the Graham company and performed for two weeks on Broadway. The spring season of 1945 at the National Theater on Broadway in New York City marked Winter's professional debut with the Graham company. Included in the season was the New York premiere of Appalachian Spring. John Martin mentioned the fine dancing by Winter as one of the Followers. Because Pearl Lang was performing in Carousel on Broadway, Winter took over her roles in Deaths and Entrances and Letter to the World. She was still a senior in college.

Upon graduation, Winter moved to New York to perform with the Graham company. She was a member of the original cast of Dark Meadow (1946) and later Night Journey (1947), and participated in the creation of these masterworks. "Miss Graham would show a piece of movement and we would have to catch it right away, without any counts. It was startling to me to see how much movement she threw away until she got exactly what she wanted." During the creation of Night Journey Ethel was introduced to the erratic temperament of Graham. "It was the opening night of Night Journey and William Schuman, the composer, was to conduct. During the afternoon rehearsal his tempos were very, very slow. Martha was just livid as it affected both the performance and the choreography. We all went to change after rehearsal and then heard this tremendous crash. Martha, without a word, had picked up the metronome and thrown it at the rehearsal accompanist. Luckily she missed!"

In October, 1945 Winter's own compositions were auditioned at the prestigious 92nd Street YM/YWHA. A performance series to showcase New York's most talented young choreographers, Winter was an "Audition Winner." She performed En Dolor, In the Clearing, and Heartbreak in the spring of 1946. Winter describes her choreography as starting from "a mood." Emotionally based and lyrical, critics praised her solo works.

Between 1944 and 1950, Winter took on many roles in the Graham company. Winter danced the role of the Spectator in Every Soul is a Circus and portrayed Pretty Polly and the Little Girl in Punch and Judy. These ballets showed Winter the comic side of Graham that many do not associate with her work. "Martha's timing and simple gestures in these works were just as strong and telling as her well-known dramatic personae. Unfortunately there is very little film footage of these great works. Martha's great versatility seems to be lost to the ages. I think it very sad that many people only connect Graham with the stark and dark." In addition to the comic pieces, Winter was in the group sections of Primitive Mysteries; in Letter to the World she learned the group sections, the Fairie Queen, and Young Love. In 1946 Winter portrayed one of the Young Girls in Deaths and Entrances and later in 1958 played a sister. She was a Follower in Appalachian Spring, and learned the group section of Diversion of Angels.

In order to make a living while dancing with the Graham Company, because "nobody made a living dancing for Martha in those days," Winter taught dance. Upon arriving in New York City, her first job was teaching tap at the YMHA and children's classes in the suburbs. Ethel then taught at the Graham School and the Neighborhood Playhouse. (Graham created her school in order to provide her dancers with much needed work.) At the Neighborhood Playhouse Graham taught students who were to become future stars - from Eli Wallach to Tony Randall. Ethel recalls working with Graham as the demonstrator at the Playhouse: "That's where Martha did some of her greatest teaching -- at the Neighborhood Playhouse. Because she had a lovely audience; they enjoyed watching her. And she taught differently there -- not that she didn't always give images and so on. But these people were able to take them further than dancers because they weren't as concerned with how it looked. They were taking it as she said it: emotionally." Winter demonstrated for Graham but often found herself teaching the class. "Of course, what happens is that you demonstrate for her about six weeks and then Martha only shows up half the time. So you end up teaching the class. But at least you've had a good background."

In 1948, Winter was the first dancer asked by Martha Graham to assume one of her roles. Graham asked Ethel to learn the solo Salem Shore for a tour with Eric Hawkins. (Until the end of her career, Graham's sentiments remained ambiguous regarding the bequeathing of roles she created for herself.) Graham relinquished roles with diffidence and scant assistance. She offered little help to Winter in the reconstruction of the solo. Taking on a Puritanical stance, Winter declared that in relinquishing the roles: "She just let you either sink or swim." In assuming Graham's roles, Winter continually triumphed.

For Salem Shore, Graham invited Winter to watch one rehearsal, and then left Ethel alone to learn the dance. Rehearsal accompanist Helen Lanfer had written extensive notes on the score, and as became tradition in reconstructing works by Graham, the musician worked extensively with Ethel to recreate the work. Graham then spent about fifteen minutes with her to polish the piece. Winter clearly "swam" because Graham asked her to perform the piece in the New York season in February before going on tour with Eric. John Martin reported that Salem Shore had previously only been danced by Miss Graham and, "It was a considerable triumph for Miss Winter, for there can be few assignments more difficult than to follow an artist of so highly personal a style. Winter looks charming, moves beautifully, and projects a wistful romanticism that is altogether in the mood of this "ballad of a woman's longing for her beloved's return from the sea"...Miss Winter is youthful, lovely and convincing, and the audience accorded her its fullest approval."

The tour with Hawkins after the New York season proved devastating to Winter. Somewhere in the middle of Iowa, the bus stalled and the battery died in the midst of a blizzard. The company (Eric Hawkins, Stuart Hodes and Winter) had to survive the night in the freezing bus before they were rescued. "Icicles were forming on the windows inside the bus and we were cold, cold, cold! We put on as much clothing and as many layers as possible." The company con-

34

tinued the tour, and Ethel developed walking pneumonia. Never fully recovering from this illness, she contracted tuberculosis.

Ethel was confined to bed rest for over a year. The therapies at the time were limited and often not effective. In 1949 while recovering, Winter was invited to return to Bennington to join the dance faculty and work towards her Masters Degree in Dance. She showed compositions under the Bennington College Dance Group at the 92nd Street Y in 1949 as a part of her Master's Project. At Bennington she met Charles Hyman, a faculty member of the Theater Arts Department, who she married in 1950 just before they left on a tour of Europe with the Graham Company. Although Charles had been in theater, Ethel and Charles knew they could not build a solid family life if they were both professional artists. Charles' father owned a trucking company, and Charles took over the family business.

During the Company tour in Europe, Graham was injured and her marriage to Hawkins began to dissolve. Winter witnessed the injury to Graham's knee. As the Spectator in Every Soul is a Circus, she was on stage when the accident took place between Graham and Hawkins. The company performed one night without Graham. They traveled to London as Graham thought a week's rest was all she needed. In dress rehearsal the knee blew up again. When she realized she would not be performing, Graham cancelled the tour. Due to previous travel arrangements, the Graham Company remained in Europe until the tour was due to conclude. Before leaving for the United States, Graham and members of the company including Ethel and Charles attended the play Venus Observed with Sir Lawrence Oliver. During the intermission, Graham searched for Hawkins. Ethel remembers Graham: "I never saw her look so defeated...She looked about two feet tall." At the conclusion of the aborted European tour, Graham stopped working with the company to recover.

Winter returned to Bennington to teach and finish her Masters degree. Unfortunately she had a relapse of tuberculosis and was confined to bed again. Doctors warned that she would never return to a career as a dancer. Winter did not relinquish hope and sought another opinion. With newly discovered medications, she was told not to give up her optimism. New therapies, strong encouragement, and dedicated care from her husband allowed Winter to believe she could return to dance.

Before taking on the rigors of Company dancing, Winter began doing shorter prestigious work. In 1951, Winter was shown in the "Dance Audition Festival" of choreographic winners from 1942 through 1950 at the 92nd Street YW/YMHA. Ethel performed in Anna Sokolow's famous Lyric Suite. Winter continued her lasting relationship with Sophie Maslow and danced as a soloist with Maslow in New York City Opera's Carmen, along with many other operas. She performed in Charles Weidman's Love of Three Oranges. In February, 1955 Ethel performed her own work at the Henry Street Playhouse, another highly selective theatre promoting new young contemporary choreographers.

In 1955 Winter decided to test her newfound stamina by taking a role as a member of the beautiful and "long legged" chorus in Ankles Aweigh. Winter followed many Graham dancers who had performed on Broadway including Pearl Lang and Yuriko. Ethel performed in Ankles Aweigh for the run of the show from April through September 1955. She worked with choreographer Tony Charmoli and briefly with Jerome Robbins who was brought in to "fix up" some of the work. "The show was fun and very challenging work. The gypsies (show dancers) love their jobs but know that if they are not dancing up to snuff they will be replaced!" Since contemporary concert dancers were forced to earn a living outside of their performing careers, Winter found the life of the gypsy easier, yet ultimately less satisfying artistically. "What was so pleasurable about being part of a show was that a dancer could earn a living doing it so at every rehearsal the cast worked at full capacity. The downside, however, can be that the show is dependent on investment money and politics which often affect the artistic integrity. Rather than "dare," they go for the "crowd pleaser" – for which I don't blame them. But it is limiting."

After establishing her regained strength with the Broadway of Ankles Aweigh, Winter auditioned for Hello Dolly and was offered a role. Ethel chose to return to the Graham Company as they were preparing for the Asian tour in 1955 and 1956. Ethel's husband, Charles, was the Stage manager for the tour. Graham's company had been chosen by the State Department and the ANTA Dance Panel to go to the Far East. Asia was considered of extreme strategic importance to the U.S. government, and the Graham Company was sent to the region to promote the U.S. through cultural exchange.

Graham and the company went abroad and conquered; the company was seen by cheering thousands. The company performed, did lecture demonstrations, and Graham gave speeches. Winter remembers: "That was a wonderful tour. Martha was incredible. She is magnificent as a speaker. Her particular kind of emotional theater was understood in Asia more than in this country – at that time. So we were really feted. We saw a great deal more of the countries and their cultures than the inside of the theater. I remember in Japan when we finished and they set off fireworks. It was really exciting. We'd never had that kind of acceptance before. It was a real privilege to be with her at that time as a part of a cultural exchange." The Asian people easily related to Graham's myths and stories. Graham told Ethel about an experience that she had in a taxi in Bangkok. The driver questioned Martha about the ballet, Cave of the Heart. Graham described Medea's anger. The taxi driver replied, "I understand that. It is like an elephant going amok!"

In addition to promoting the U.S. as a cultural center with the creation of new dance forms, Graham was sent to Asia in an effort to enhance the image of the U.S. as a racially integrated country according to Naima Prevots in Dance for Export. As the communists used the growing strains of U.S. race relations, Graham's integrated company showed the U.S. at its best. Graham's approach to the integration of her company impressed Winter. She believes that Graham's deep integrity in her treatment of people was unique for the time: "Martha had a mixture of people in her company long before anybody said, "Oh, you've got to have people of color." She didn't think that way at all. I mean, if you had talent, she was interested in you. Martha was really very forward thinking. I think she deserves a lot of credit. She took a person as a person. It didn't matter what their color was." Winter remembers that Graham took Yuriko into the company during WWII when Japanese descendents were in Internment Camps in the U.S. The Company was touring in the South and Winter remembers that there was no African American member of the company yet, but Yuriko was there. "We were in a train station, and one sign said "For Whites" and one said "For Blacks" and Yuriko said to me, "Where do I go?" And it was very confusing, and upsetting to say the least. So later Martha just wouldn't tour to some places that were not accepting of Blacks. In other words, some Southern cities: she just wouldn't go there until the laws changed." Winter states: "You know, she wasn't shouting her politics, but she was sticking by what she believed."

Graham was chosen by the government to go to Asia due to her commitment to equality, yet in Asia Graham was challenged on just these grounds. Graham was asked by the press why there were no dances about universal brotherhood. Graham responded, "There are no dances in my company in which that is not the subject...I don't need to make dances that say they are about brotherhood. All of my dances are." Winter remembers the following: "When we were in India, some reporters got hold of them (the African American members of the Company), and wanted to know if they were treated any differently than the rest of the Company. And I just found that absurd, in terms of us, because we all never thought of it." She found it incongruous that the reporters in India, steeped in a rigid class caste system, would challenge the integrated Company.

After returning from the triumphant Asian tour, Ethel and Charles wanted to establish their own home in New York with studio space for both of them. Although an active member of the Company, Winter always strove to keep her private life private. "One thing I realized after witnessing company members with psychological bruises was that it was better to keep one's personal life separate from work." Since Ethel and Charles sought to create a home with unique space, and apartments did not accommodate their needs, they searched for a house. They found one in Manhattan, and with Charles' expertise as a designer and craftsman, they demolished the inside and renovated the townhouse on their own. They filed plans and reported to the Department of Buildings that they would be doing the construction themselves. One afternoon an inspector came to their door. Ethel had been ripping the old plaster off the walls, and was covered from head to toe in dust. The inspector did not need much convincing to believe that the report filed was wholly accurate. Winter reported that getting to rehearsals free of plaster and paint was a feat for several years. Their long labors served them well, and the house is still their home today. Now they rent the larger portion of the house, and enjoy plantings and gardening in their backyard just off the ground floor that they occupy.

In 1958, their son David was born. Remarkably, in the same year Winter performed with the Graham Company in the spring and was given glowing reviews in existing roles, and in the new Clytemnestra in which she created the role of Helen of Troy. After David's birth, the family often joined Winter as she traveled on tour and to teach. Yet Ethel felt the modern strains of balancing a family and a professional career. She remembers wonderful moments such as taking her son to Israel when he was five and having Bethsabee de Rothschild take them to the beach on Sundays. David regularly came to rehearsals and sat under the piano coloring and watching the dancers rehearse. "He was probably the only five-year-old who could sing parts of Clytemnestra." Years later when Ethel told her son that she was retiring from the Graham Company he replied with disappointment: "Does that mean we won't be traveling anymore?" The guilt Winter had occasionally felt about uprooting her family for her career was allayed.

The late 1950s and 1960s marked an apex of Winter's career. The Graham Company was at an artistic peak, and Graham was creating new works as well as reviving older repertory pieces for Broadway seasons. Written under a picture of Winter portraying the Bride, the New York Times proclaimed: "Graham has established her right to be regarded as one of the great choreographers of our time." Although Graham was difficult to work under, the results were magnificent. Winter remembers: "Martha was a hard taskmaster. When she was at her most creative, tempers were frayed and she would become so frustrated that in her fury she would attack the dancers verbally and say she never wanted to see us again and to just leave. The Company would go to the dressing room and wait. Later Martha would come back like an apologetic little girl and ask forgiveness. She was a very human being!" Yet through all the turmoil, John Martin spoke of the dancers saying they: "encroach on the miraculous." He continued later: "And what a company (Miss Graham) has assembled and built over the years! They are not only extraordinarily handsome to look at, but can move with a physical command and a common purpose that make for something very close to perfection."

Winter was consistently cited as an outstanding member of the Graham Company and was referred to by John Martin as one of the "truly great dancers." As in the 1940s, Winter was again asked by Graham to learn her roles that had never before been danced by other Company members: She took over Graham's part in Herodiade and Frontier. As became standard, Ethel was responsible for reconstructing the choreography through film, memory, and with the assistance of the rehearsal accompanist. In the reconstruction of Frontier for the Louis Horst retrospective in 1964, Graham had ambivalent feelings about showing the work choreographed in the 1930s. Ethel believes that Graham did not want to look dated: she wanted to look forward. Frontier was particularly difficult because no one had seen the dance, and the only existing film was made to document the set. The music and the dance were out of sync. Winter recollects: "There were some notations on the musical score, and that's how I knew that the film wasn't in synch. But it was like a crossword puzzle to make things fit." Graham reviewed the reconstruction only after the work was done. In the case of Frontier, "only for ten minutes." Ethel's approach to the reconstruction was pragmatic and professional. She says: "Martha gave you the script, and you had to do something with it." Winter was also challenged in the reconstruction of other works, but appreciated the polishing work Graham offered. "I know in doing Herodiade, Martha came in for maybe fifteen minutes, and those fifteen minutes were fabulous. What she could give you in that short time was really incredible. Because she wasn't saying: "You have to turn out here." It was the essence of the movement." Ethel's performances in these reconstructions were so memorable that they were recalled years later by reviewers. In 1999 Jack Anderson remembers the 1964 performance of Frontier: "I was thrilled by the way Ethel Winter kept kicking her leg with a pioneer woman's determination."

Winter assumed and shared leading roles with other company members such as the Bride in Appalachian Spring, the Woman in Red in Diversions of Angels, Joan in Seraphic Dialogue, Matt Turney's role in Part Real, Part Dream, and Jocasta in Night Journey. Winter had performed in Appalachian Spring since college as one of the Followers. She says: "I loved Appalachian Spring. I loved the music. And of course it's very close to so much of my upbringing. So I always loved doing the role of the Bride. When I was given the chance to do the role, it was not that difficult because I had sat on that bench so many times watching Martha do her solos. I felt very at home in that role." In performing Appalachian Spring, she describes the task of taking on Graham's roles by equating Graham's ballets to great plays. Winter never tried to become Graham or imitate her; she used the dance to elicit her character. "I just did the role of the Bride very simply. That this was a young girl in love! And I

40

suppose it depends on how you look at the whole world. That we should be a loving community. Martha was trying for that, but she was a different person. You go and see Hamlet and there are different people doing the same lines, but they're different: that's all. Because of my background, I think I probably felt the role in a simpler way." The critics adored Winter. Martin titled her depiction "magnificent," and continued: "Ethel Winter danced with a sharp, alert brightness, darting happily inside the choreography." Clive Barnes said, "While the Bride is made as fresh and young as ever, Winter gives the role a new quality of hardness, a hint of endurance beneath the bridal floss."

Winter danced the Girl in Red in Diversions of Angels and was called "spectacular" by reviewers. Partnered with Robert Cohan, they depicted "discovering love and movement as though for the first time." Again, Ethel's love of the music and the work itself inspired her many notable performances. Her reviews were consistently spectacular. As Joan the Maid In Seraphic Dialogue and the New York Times called her "radiant and universal," and "eloquent." The press report of Graham's European tour in the summer of 1963 includes the headline: "Ethel Winter Acclaimed'" The article continues to herald Winter's fine performance in Edinburgh.

As Jocasta in Night Journey, Winter was "totally different" from Graham according to Clive Barnes. He wrote: "Miss Winter, naturally, goes her own way." He continued: "Miss Winter is full of blood and full of life." Although Winter used warmth to color the character, Barnes found the shift effective. He concluded: "This is what we need in our day and age – a Jocasta to submerge with an abstracted yet decent gesture of human impotence, rather than a proudly tragic furl of heroic satiation. Miss Winter, feminine and frustrated, is a Jocasta for our times."

In Clytemnestra, created on Winter, she was charged with portraying the lovely Helen of Troy. Of her dramatic moments with Graham on stage Winter remembers: "We looked each other in the eye in Clytemnestra, that's for sure. Because I always did things as an actress, just as Martha did, and we both had venom in our eyes! She was strong. But, for me it was helpful. You play better tennis if you get a better tennis player." Winter recalls: "It's funny, Martha always wanted to be known as a dancer, and I think of her more as an actress. A dancer, yes, but an actress dancer." One reviewer recalls:

"In Clytemnestra Winter found that she spontaneously pitched her own performance to the intensity of Martha's mood in a highly charged scene. Due to the younger artist's exquisite sense of timing, the drama inherent in the encounter was invariably held at the point of extreme tension. Such sensitivity was characteristic of Winter."

In Graham's works, Winter had always been charged with the lyric and innocent roles, yet one incident shifted Graham's perception of her and led the way for Winter's role as Aphrodite in Phaedra. During the Asian tour, Winter danced the role of Dawn in Ardent Song. "Dawn should have been glowing and sparkly, but on this one evening everything went wrong. It was 110 degrees and my costume was drenched. There were missed cues, and props went awry. Material that I should have twirled, ended up tangled around my ankles instead of around my waist." In the dressing room, Winter ripped off her costume and threw it on the dirt floor. To the surprise of the Company, she began stamping on the dress and swearing uncharacteristically. Winter had forgotten that Miss Graham herself was sharing the dressing room, and when Ethel looked up, Martha's eyes were on her. Although she thought Graham would not be pleased with her behavior, Graham simply stared and said empathically "Good girl, Ethel." After this episode, Graham created the role of Aphrodite for Winter. Her untouchable range became a signature of her career. The New York Times said: "Ethel Winter makes Aphrodite permeating vulgar and vicious, though half an hour earlier she was the most beautiful and heartbreaking Joan of Arc in Seraphic Dialogue." Winter also partnered Paul Taylor in the creation of Cleopatra to his Antony in One More Gaudy Night. Paul Taylor writes in his autobiography: "Ethel Winter is a many pointed star – spiritual as St. Joan, lascivious as Aphrodite, flirtatious as Cleopatra – variable according to how she is cast. Though Ethel's portrayals demonstrate her talent for varied roles, her individuality always comes through clearly." The last role that Graham created for Winter was Andromache in Cortege of Eagles in 1967. As Graham's health deteriorated due to complications surrounding alcohol abuse, the rehearsals became time consuming and offered little reward. "It was a painful struggle for all involved. Martha always changed and discarded sections, but this time it was just plain fussing. The Company all tried to be helpful, but it seemed that her concentration was blurred. Her critical eye was just not in focus."

During the late 1950s and 1960s, Graham created many group works that included Winter such as Episodes (1959), Acrobats of God (1960), and Alcestis (1960). Of the group works, Episodes was most notable in the press as it marked a collaboration between two of the era's great choreographers: Graham and George Balanchine. Although billed as a collaboration, observers saw it as little more than music shared. Paul Taylor referred to the piece akin to "His and Hers towels." Winter remembers: "The wonderful thing about Episodes was that we were in period dress, so to speak. Martha certainly was. And the Balanchine group was in just leotards and tights and no shoes. I had gone to see Melissa Hayden in Medea, and I sat in front, and I heard this conversation behind me. One person said, "Well, now, how will I know which is the modern section and which is the ballet? I mean, will I like it?" They were talking about Episodes. The other woman said, "Oh, well, you can't help but tell, because the ones with Graham will be without shoes and sparse costumes." And it was just completely the opposite, so I thought that was rather amusing. It was a good ploy for both modern and ballet, because it got a section of people coming to see one thing, and another section to see another: it broadened the audience, you know. I think it was good PR. I do think (Miss Graham and Balanchine) respected the other one in what they did. But, I don't think they intended to really collaborate."

The public's great interest in the dance was met by several films made of the Graham Company. In 1957, Winter participated in the making of Martha Graham's film A Dancer's World and performed as one of the Followers in Appalachian Spring in 1959. In A Dancer's World, Winter is featured with other members of the company. Ethel says, "I wasn't in on it from the beginning because I was off doing summer stock. There, I wore the Hope Diamond to publicize the theatre. Nobody would wear it because of bad luck. And I said, "Oh, that's ridiculous." So I wore it, and don't you know that the next rehearsal I broke my foot. But I was lucky. We were out in nowhere, and at the hospital a surgeon took care of me. He was marvelous. I said, "Gee, I can't imagine you giving such care." And he said, "Well, just think, I'm a surgeon. If I cut my hand, I wouldn't be able to operate. You're a dancer: you've got to use your foot." I came back to do the movie. I was glad to be able to be part of that. It's amazing. It's so simply done. And yet I think it's really quite telling."

To provide more performing opportunities, Winter formed her dance company in 1962. She toured throughout the Eastern United States from 1962 through 1969 to great critical acclaim. Ethel remembers touring in a station wagon and feeling as though "every University is at the top of a mountain." In 1964, the press reported that Winter's New York season at the 92nd Street Y was a huge success. "It was headed by a star of the Martha Graham Dance Company, Ethel Winter, who serves as chief choreographer of the five-member ensemble. Of the six works on the program, two were solos created and danced by Miss Winter. One of the four group works was choreographed by Sophie Maslow. The solos provided the finest moments of the evening, partly because Winter is a beautiful dancer in every respect, partly because the choreography of the pieces was notably good." Over the years, Ethel discovered and nurtured fine dancers who went on to join the companies of Paul Taylor, Glen Tetley, Pearl Lang, and Mary Anthony. Ethel designed her own costumes and Charles designed the sets. She preferred to use original music, and collaborated with several composers such as Joseph Liebling (Suite of Three), Eugene Lester (Night Forrest), Arthur Murphy (The Magic Mirror) and Gwen Watson (Two Shadows Passed). In addition, Ethel choreographed to the existing scores of Paul Bowles (Fun and Fancy) and Manuel De Falla (En Dolor). Walter Sorrell said of her solos: "She is a dancer with tremendous range of expressiveness, with depth in her characterization and an awareness for the finest nuances."

Although Winter loved performing and enjoyed choreographing solo works, she disbanded the company after seven seasons. Because the dancers were constantly leaving for larger companies, resetting the works with new dancers became very time consuming. Winter concludes: "I think you have to really have a burning desire to be a choreographer. I really enjoyed being an actress, to take a role and make it mine. This I enjoyed more than writing the script."

Besides her flourishing career with Graham, Winter engaged in work with other companies and venues. She continued her work with Sophie Maslow performing in the legendary The Village I Knew as well as in the magnificent Chanukah Festivals at Madison Square Garden. In a review of the festival, Clive Barns said: "Ethel Winter (someone should call her the Winter of our Content) was splendidly lithe and sinuous." Winter performed often with The

Group Dance Theater, headed by Maslow. Originating the role of Leah in Neither Rest Nor Harbor based on The Dybbuk, the New York Times said, " What is outstanding is the performance by Miss Winter as Leah...she brings to the role her unusual mixture of serenity, grace and spiritual force. Her dancing has an eloquence of its own." In addition, Winter joined Yuriko and her company to dance in The Ghost, originating the role of the Bride. Winter made her television debut on Mister Roger's Neighborhood. She recalls: "I had never seen the Mr. Rogers show because my son had already grown up. So I watched it and thought, "Oh my goodness, this is so slow. I'm going to speed it up a bit." But it seemed they only had one camera, so if you went too fast the camera couldn't follow you. And he said to me, "You have to go slower." And I just thought that was a hoot. I remember I had made up this little story that I danced about a princess, and I said something about being afraid. And he said, "Oh no. No, you can't use that word." So we had to change that word. He was really very careful about what he presented to children – he wanted to relax them."

Winter taught dance extensively. Besides her teaching at the Graham School, Winter taught at the prestigious Juilliard School. At Juilliard her students called her "The Happy Contraction Lady" due to her joyous yet highly disciplined approach. She says: "Because I used to make them laugh. That's why: "HA!" rather than "huh." You laugh from your gut just as much as you cry from your gut. And I found more success with younger people if you laughed. And after getting a sensation of it, then you can get them into different modes. We have a vocabulary in words, and we don't always say them the same way, so why do you have to think that a contraction is only one thing? It's many things." She continued, saying that she tries to cajole the tension and timidity out of dancers. Winter said of teaching the technique: "Martha's technique comes from inside to get to the outside, not from the outside to get to the inside. And that's what's hard about it. But that's what's so rewarding, because you find something different in it all the time." At Juilliard, Winter choreographed and reset pieces for the Juilliard Dance Ensemble. Her Juilliard work, The Magic Mirror, included Kazuko Hirabayashi and Linda Shoop. She gained rave reviews for her staging of Diversion of Angels at the school in 1993. Ethel retired from Juilliard in 2003.

During the 1960s there were several ventures to establish training centers for Graham technique throughout the world. In 1963, Winter was invited by Bethsabee de Rothschild to become a founding teacher and choreographer in Israel when the Batsheva Dance Company was being established. Winter accepted and set her Fun and Fancy on the new company and trained the dancers in the Graham technique. In 1964, Robin Howard asked Winter, Mary Hinkson and Bertram Ross to teach in London. Their work provided the impetus for their now legendary London School of Contemporary Dance. They came as pioneers to teach the technique and educate audiences in small communities around London through shared performances with the second company of the Royal Ballet. Ethel remembers one rehearsal: "At the Hammerstein Theater we were rehearsing for a lecture demonstration and we asked Mr. Howard if he would mind getting us some lunch. Now as dancers from the States, we were only expecting a sandwich or a hamburger. But he returned an hour later, much to our surprise, with a large basket filled with fancy china, and silver place settings for six, and an incredible gourmet picnic!" The group was an extraordinary success, and the London Contemporary Dance Theater was launched.

In the late 1960s, Winter was selected as the first dancer in the Affiliate Artist Program, an organization that sent prominent artists to small colleges to teach, perform, and serve as ambassadors for the promotion of contemporary art to the public. Over four years, Winter gave lecture demonstrations, taught, and performed her own choreography at myriad institutions throughout the United States. She participated in the program's Beloit Festival in Wisconsin during which the artists cam together and performed. There she choreographed and performed her solo Barbara Allen Ballad. She also choreographed the opening number from Hair titled "Aquarius," and show numbers for Diamonds are a Girl's Best Friend and Watching All the Gills Go By.

Winter retired from performing in 1969. She gave her final performance as Joan of Arc in Seraphic Dialogue. Ethel returned several times until 1973 as a guest artist. Although Graham was difficult to work for, Winter carries an enduring respect for the artist: "Martha had her own particular genius. Movement was communication to her, not just putting steps together." The decision to stop performing was a major change in her life. "I didn't mind teaching my roles.

I loved it, but it was hard not to perform any longer. I thought that teaching would completely take its place but it didn't totally. It was like losing a dear friend."

The years between Winter's departure from the Graham Company and her return as the Director of the School at the Martha Graham Center of Contemporary Dance in 1973 were legendary as a time of great upheaval for the organization. After recovering from a protracted illness, Graham returned with Ron Protas at her side. Many of Graham's leading core members were forced to leave the company including Mary Hinkson and Bertram Ross. After a five year performing hiatus for the company on Broadway, Winter helped to reconstruct pieces for the Graham Company's 1974 Broadway season.

In 1993, Winter said, "I am the latest to be banned from the Graham studio." After coaching Joyce Herring in Seraphic Dialogue, she went backstage to congratulate her on the performance and suggest a few improvements. Mr. Protas was lurking about and stated that he didn't agree, and was going to tell Herring that she didn't do well. With only the three people in the room, Winter asked him specifically about his criticism and this evidently made him furious. The next day after she had finished teaching class at the Graham School, and with numerous students milling through the hall, Protas accosted Ethel in the hallway. He said, "Don't you ever criticize me in public again." Ethel returned the reprimand: "Don't you ever criticize me in public." Protas rejoined, "Leave and don't ever come back." Winter replied, "I won't," and that was that. "I was so livid. You don't get paid for your time teaching somebody. I wasn't trying to take any glory away from him; I just wanted the part to be done well."

Yet in Ethel's signature pragmatic style, she understood the relationship of Graham to Protos. She says: "From the point of view her recovery the last time, you have to give credit to Protas. He got her back. And if he'd just taken care of her as he started out to do that would've been wonderful, but then he tried to get into the whole artistic thing. I was sorry that Martha was taken in by him. I would not be a part of that. But I will give him credit for getting her back to work." After Protas was removed by the Graham Board of Directors, Winter returned to teach advanced classes and remains a favorite teacher.

Winter continued her devotion to teaching and acted as ambassador for American contemporary dance after her retirement from the stage. Her teaching assignments took her around the U.S. and the world. In 1974 she taught at the Southwest Festival with Arthur Mitchell and David Howard with over 900 dancers and concerts that sold over 11,400 tickets. She has been a guest teacher at centers throughout the US including the summer school at Connecticut College, The New World School of Arts in Miami, Philadenco Dance Company, and the Repertory Dance Theater of Utah. In 1983 she was invited by David Gayle, director of the Ilkley Ballet Seminar, to come to England as a guest teacher. She spent a month in Yorkshire presenting lectures, demonstrations and teaching master classes at many schools, colleges, universities and dance centers throughout the region. During the trip, Yair Varadi, Director of the English Dance Theater, invited her to teach at his two-week summer intensive at the Darlington Arts Center. Winter returned for the following two years and set her solo, En Dolor, on one of his dancers to celebrate the opening of their new center in Newcastle. She also enjoyed her twelve year relationship with the Akar Modern Dance Studio in Bern, Switzerland.

Winter is recognized as a brilliant and versatile dancer, an inspirational and disciplined mentor for students, and a choreographer of critical acclaim. Her career is marked by recognition of professional dance organizations which value her intelligence, insights, and knowledge. She has been a judge for the Massachusetts Arts Council, the New York State Dance Council, the Southwest Regional Ballet Association, and has served as a member of the Dance Panel for the National Endowment for the Arts.

Although Winter claims that "words have never been easy for me," her gracious and articulate thoughts are self evident when she speaks. Asked what inspires her work she replies: "The arts, poetry, literature and music." It is worth reiterating her strong feelings about dance today: "I am worried about the fact that we are in a computer age and everybody is doing everything by the numbers. I am worried about the humanity and the spirit. I think dance has that particular quality that can project the spirit. When I see things that are just athletic, technical, and beautifully done, it just doesn't grab me. I'd rather see someone working from the heart." However, she adds: "I do love the circus."

Photographies

Ethel Winter
Photography by Charles Hyman
Courtesy of the photographer

Ehtel Winter as Herodiade, 1963
Photography by Oleago
Courtesy of the photographer

Ethel Winter as Joan in Seraphic Dialogue, 1958.
Photography by Joyce Noyes.
Courtesy of the photographer.

Ethel Winter, Moss Cohen, Poems in The Magic Mirror, 1961.
Photography by Joyce Noyes.
Courtesy of the photographer.

Ethel Winter in Jane Dudly's Harmonica Breakdown, 1970.
Photography by Betty Jones.
Courtesy of the photographer.

Ethel Winter, Moss Cohen in Two Shadows Passed, 1961.
Photography by Jim A. Langley.
Courtesy of the photographer.

Ethel Winter in Martha Graham's Salem Shore, 1948.
Photography by Fred Fehl
Courtesy of the photographer

Ethel Winter in Suite of Three, 1961.
Photography by Jim A. Langley
Courtesy of the photographer

Ethel Winter in One and Lost
(also called Night Conversations), 1968.
Photography by Jim A. Langley
Courtesy of the photographer

Ethel Winter, Wesley Fata (behind) in Night Forest, 1962
Photography by Jack Mitchell
Courtesy of Ethel Winter

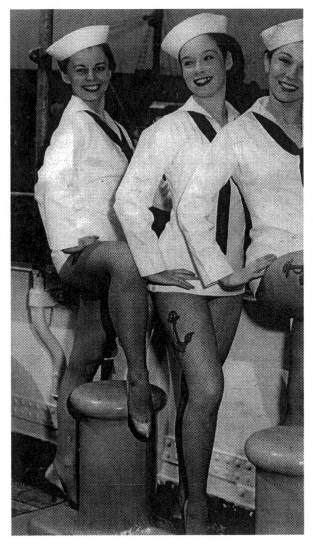

Ethel Winter, Sandy Bonner, Meri Miller (from left to right),
Broadway show Ankles Away, 1954
Photography: newspaper

Ethel Winter as Liat, Margaret Tyne (center), Richard Amburster,
South Pacific – summer stock, 1957
Photography: newspaper

EN DOLOR

Ethel Winter in En Dolor (early costume), 1961
Photography by Jim A. Langley
Courtesy of the photographer

En Dolor

Introduction

En Dolor has been described as "a lament of memory". The piece portrays a woman mourning a personal loss and she must deal with her grief and anger.

Creation

Ethel Winter choreographed En Dolor in 1944 at the age of 19 during her dance studies at Bennington College. One of her earliest solos, the initial inspirations for the piece came after Ethel had been reading about the Spanish Civil War. While in a music seminar class she heard Pantomime, a section from the DeFalla Opera El Amor Brujo. She fell in love with it instantly. Some years later however, upon hearing this section played as orchestrated, she was shocked to find the quality so different from what she had felt when listening to the piano scoring.

En Dolor reveals Ethel Winter's early dance background in Spanish Dance and Ballet. She comments, "I had just enough Graham training that I was able to use the quality of the strong spine needed for the character of the solo." The solo she says, "is really a mixture of the three styles: Spanish, Ballet and a layer of Graham." The solo was performed for the first time at the annual student dance concert at Bennington College. When Louis Horst, Martha Graham's musical director, first saw Ethel performing En Dolor he was very impressed and said to Martha Graham "take her."

Development

Ethel Winter performed En Dolor many times during the years she had her own company and as an Affiliate. The solo choreographed in A, B, A form continued to develop over time. When asked how the solo has changed, Ethel replied, "It became much deeper over the years." At a later point, Ethel began to teach the solo to her dance students at Juilliard for repertory workshops. En Dolor has also been set on professional dancers Stella Mae of the English Dance Theatre in 1984 and Karin Hermes who performed the solo in 2001 for the Akar Werkstatt project

Interpretation

On the question of what is important for the interpretation of the solo, Ethel replied "Now I have a story for the solo but I didn't when I first choreographed it. What is important to me is that the solo is a character that is strong and proud. The spine tells you this. The dance has to do with not giving up, not giving into one's emotions." She goes on to say "this character must be a woman, (not a girl) who perhaps, has lost a son."

In the first section, one sees the anger and grief of the woman's personal loss. Then there is a transition into the second section where the woman tries to remember and relive a happier time. "The woman is trying to dance again but never can quite make it. That is why in the very last section, the piece does become positive. Even though the woman has this anger and sadness, it will not conquer her. She will go on."

Motifs

Throughout the solo there is an interesting hip movement that repeats in different variations as one of the basic motifs. When asked if there was any particular meaning for the repeated hip movement, Ethel replied, "Well, I once had somebody tell me that dancers never seem to move their hips (which is not so today)." Here she is referring to the fact that traditionally classical dance did not commonly use isolated hip movements, so Ethel took upon the challenge to incorporate meaningful hip movements into the solo. The hip movement combined with contractions in the pelvis, Ethel explains, should express the feeling of a "little cry" as the qualities of pain and grief are really felt in the gut.

Final Remarks

En Dolor has a very special meaning for Ethel. She lost a lot of her other solo works over the years but this one has always stayed with her. "I think I didn't lose this solo because it can have meaning for so many people. Very few individuals can escape the tragedy of personal loss."

Rehearsal notes

The expressions Ethel used in rehearsals are written in quotation marks in the score.

What I remember most about rehearsing with Ethel is her demanding: „attack more" and „attack sharper". She even asked this when I felt that I attacked strongly. From my perspective today I think I did not enough understand the strong impulse from the centre which is at the same time in the whole body. The movements have to be clear, direct and strong. No floating. Not lyric. The body is very pulled up.

Starting position: it helps to think about a diagonal pull upwards in the upper body.

Measure 5 / count 1: (Arm circle): „Wild", „hit", „swearing"

Measure 5 /count 2-3, Measure 78-79: be aware that in this holding contraction the pelvis and shoulders should be well placed above each other (often the upper body tends to be too much forward)

Measures 6-7: First backwards steps: they repeat often throughout the dance: if you learn or teach them: think about kicking the skirt

Measures 11-14: the feeling of "spiraling down"

Measure 19 / count 1, Measure22 / count 1, Measure 89 /count 4,5, Measure 91 / count 1,2: rising on "demi-pointe" (high level): start it in the back: the back changes with attack and that energy pulls you right up to rise on "demi-pointe".

Measure: 42-43: "trying to escape the pain", "smooth"

Measures 84-90: On this "2nd diagonal": chin a little higher than on the 1st diagonal in measures 17-23.

Measure 85: Standing seems long for dancer, but has to be kept: is very powerful. Very uplifted upper body: "strong", "proud", decision to go on in life

Measure 72 / count 2, 3: On knee absolute still: keep the pause

Musical interpretation

If you perform with a live pianist: consider enough time to rehearse tempi and dynamics as Ethel wants them. They are NOT as written in the musical score. Please consult the rehearsal tape. Ethel wants the musical interpretation with insistence. If a mature performer with strong personality is performing: the diagonals (measures 17 – 23 and measures 84 – 90) can be very slow.

Technical Glossary

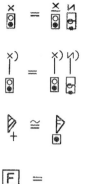   "Graham Contraction"

deepening of "Graham Contraction"

slightly side high movement is initiated by the right hip (same applies to the left side)

F =   Floor

measure 65 :

possible variation for right arm movement :

measure 42 :

 can also be 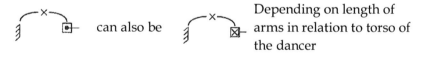 Depending on length of arms in relation to torso of the dancer

measures 48 – 50 :

If necessary for spacing: flat diagonal upstage

Score

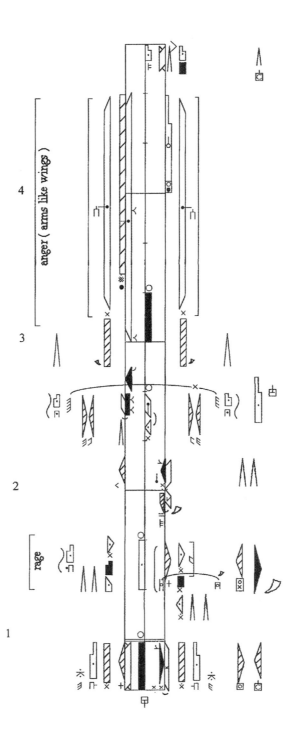

anger (arms like wings)

4

3

rage

2

1

$\quad\bullet\ =$

m $\sim$ 132

3 2 7 6
4 4 8 8

(KIN)

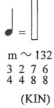

69

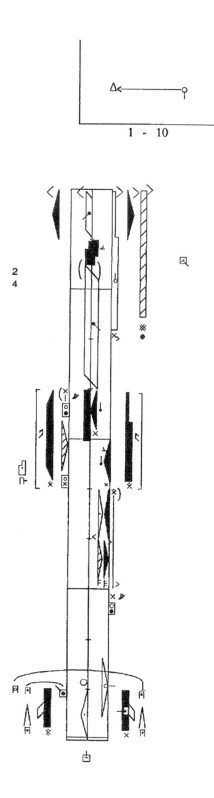

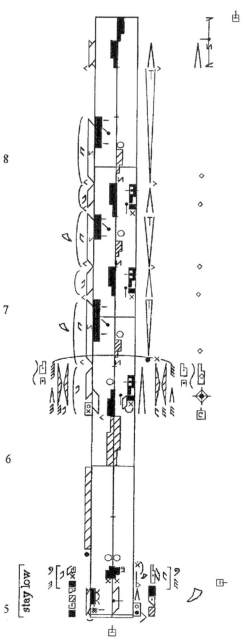

1 - 10

5   stay low

6

7

8

9

10

11

12

2
4

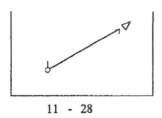

11 - 28

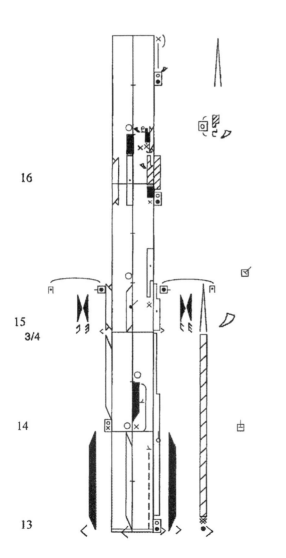

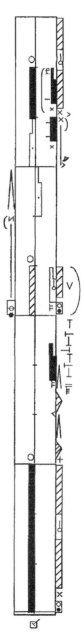

16

15
3/4

14

13

20

19

18

17

71

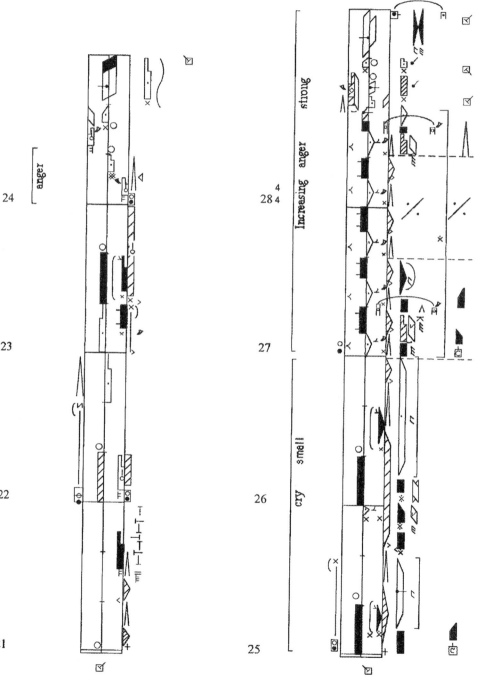

anger

cry   small   increasing anger   rising

21   22   23   24

25   26   27   28

4
4

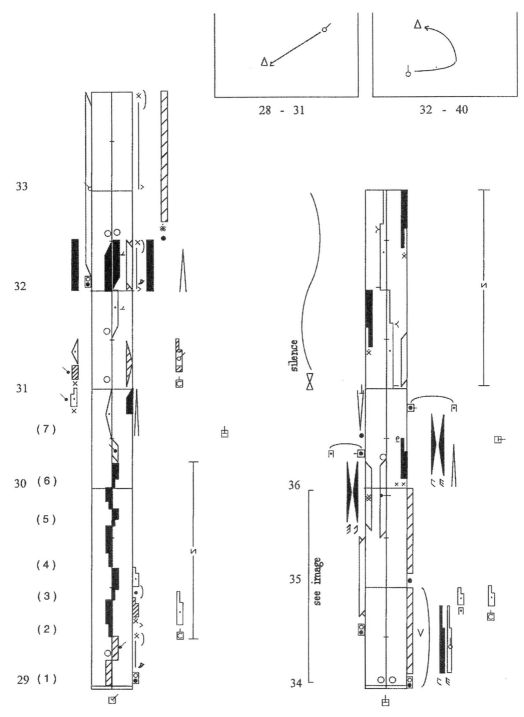

28 - 31

32 - 40

33

32

31

(7)

30 (6)

(5)

(4)

35 (3)

(2)

29 (1)

silence

36

35

see image

34

73

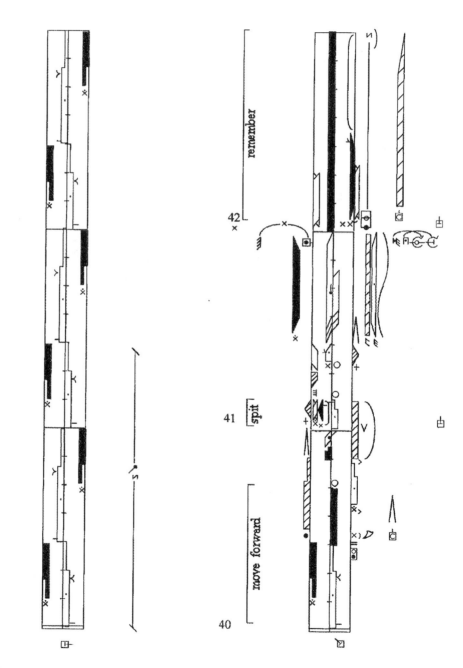

39

38

37   7
      8

42 ⌐
    remember
    ×

41 ⌐ spit

40

move forward

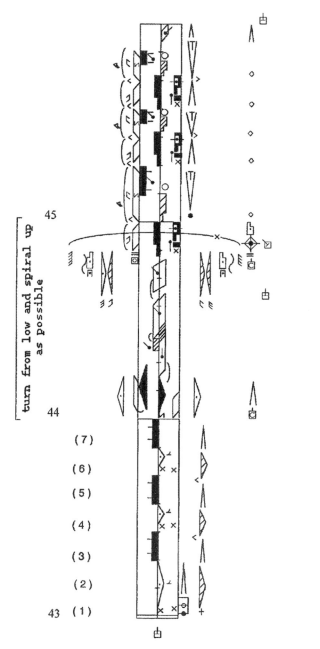

45

44

43 (1)
(2)
(3)
(4)
(5)
(6)
(7)

turn from low and spiral up
as possible

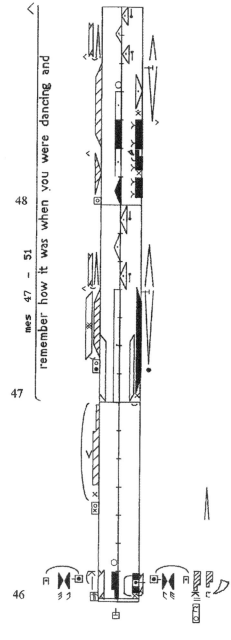

48

47

46

mes 47 – 51
remember how it was when you were dancing and

75

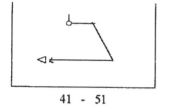

41 - 51

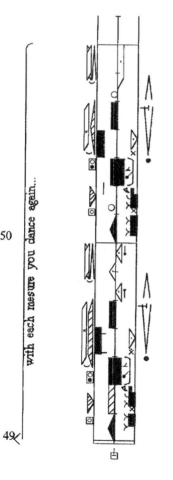

50

49

with each mesure you dance again...

53

52

51

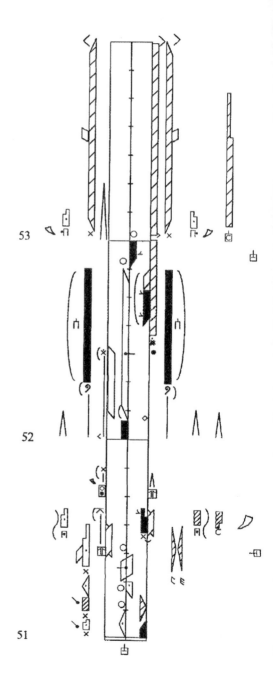

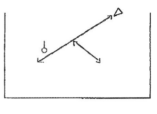

52 - 60

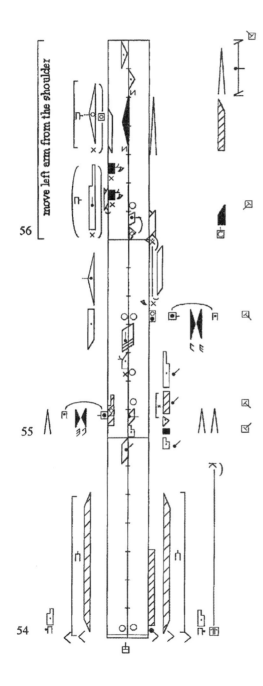

move left arm from the shoulder

56

55

54

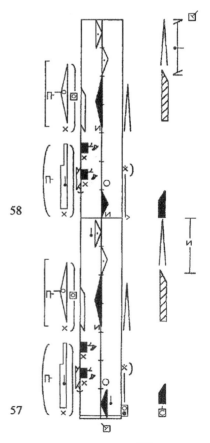

58

57

77

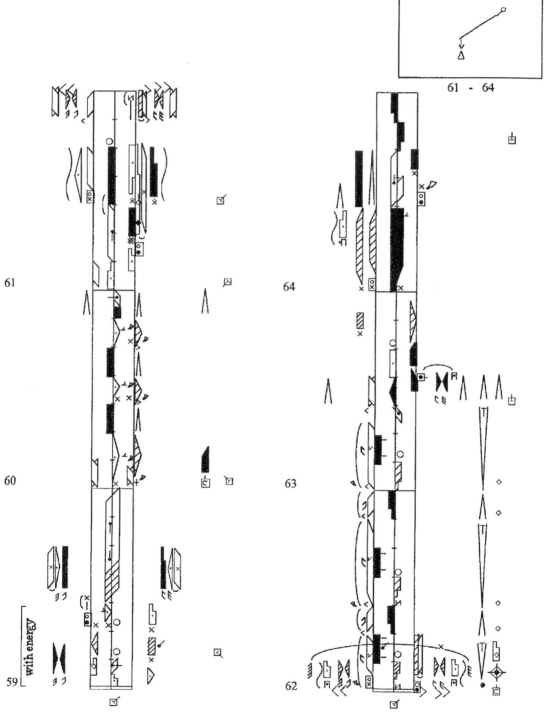

61 - 64

64

61

63

60

62

59

with energy

78

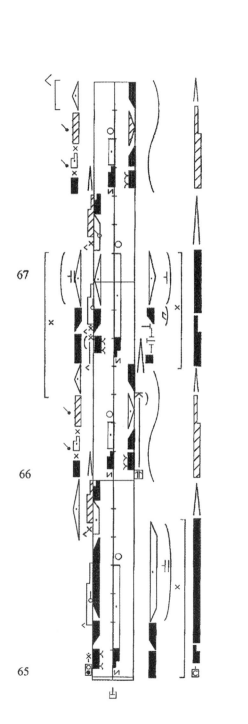

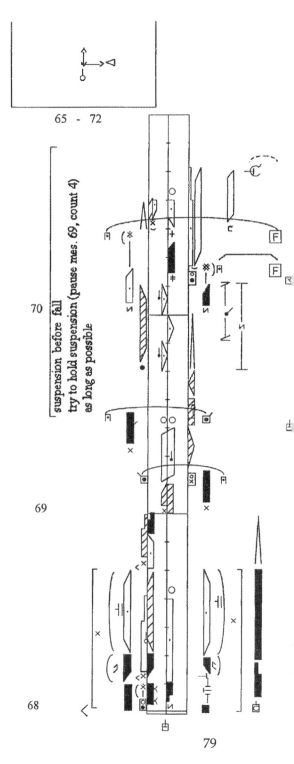

67

66

65

70

69

68

suspension before fall
try to hold suspension (pause mes. 69, count 4)
as long as possible

79

73 - 78

73

72

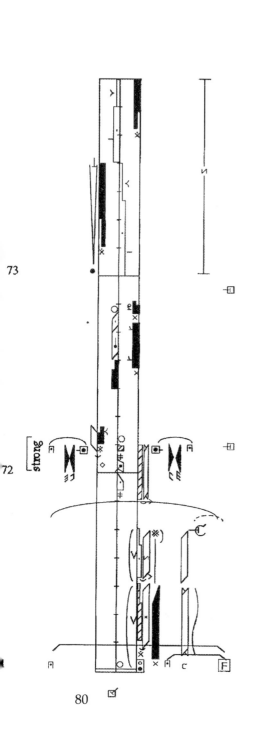

80

76

75 6/8

74

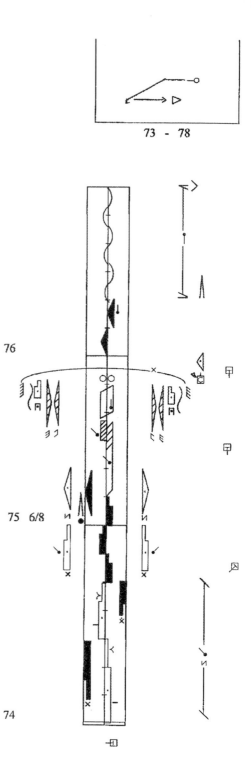

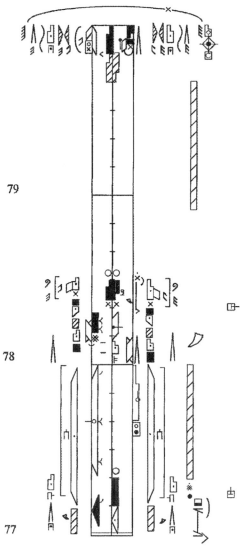

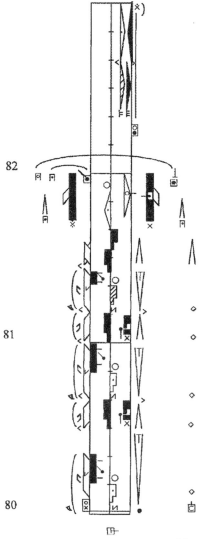

79

82

78

81

77

80

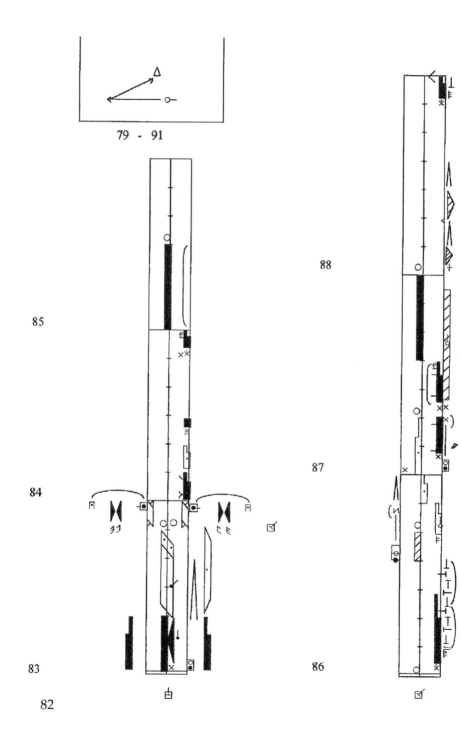

79 - 91

85

84

83

82

88

87

86

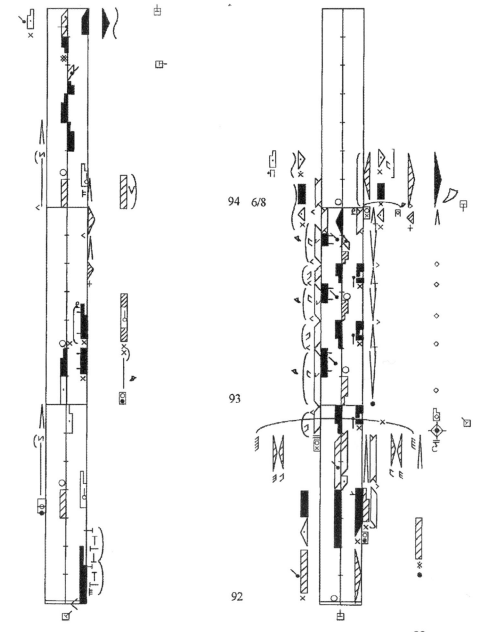

91

94 6/8

90

93

89

92

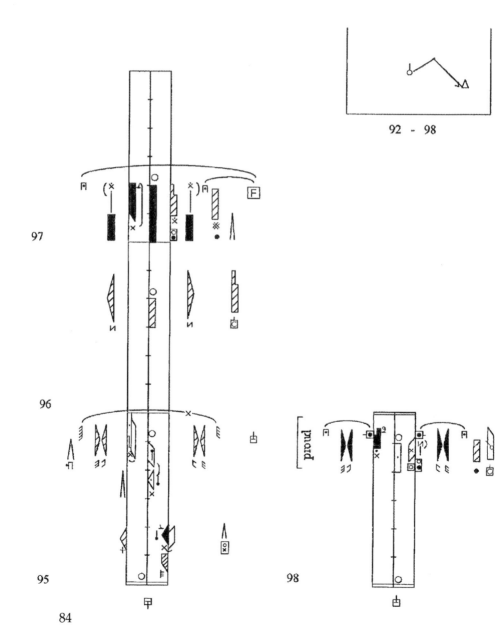

92 - 98

Floorplans

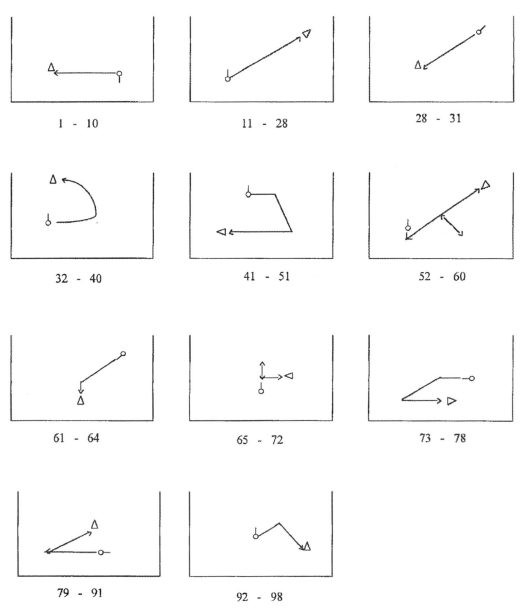

1 - 10

11 - 28

28 - 31

32 - 40

41 - 51

52 - 60

61 - 64

65 - 72

73 - 78

79 - 91

92 - 98

APPENDIX

Excerpts from the Press

The following excerpts from the Press are a selection of hundreds of articles from newspaper and magazines from all over the world; collected by Charles Hyman.

Salem Shore Role Danced by Winter: "Those of us who are familiar with Miss Graham's own performance of it will perhaps never be content with anything else, for that smoldering inwardness is hard to equal and these characteristic Graham intransigencies of movement are virtually impossible for another dancer to justify. Nevertheless, Miss Winter is youthful, lovely and convincing, and the audience accorded her its fullest approval."

By John Martin, New York Times, Feb. 27, 1948.

"Miss Winter touches the part with gentle anguish and her day dreams are marked by a wonderful joyous spirit, by a wide-eyed innocence which is dewy fresh. If her interpretation does not seem to go as deeply into emotional compulsions as does that of Miss Graham, it is, nevertheless, compelling in its very youthfulness."

(Ethel Winter presents Role of Wife in Salem Shore)

By Walter Terry, New York Herald Tribune, Feb. 26, 1948.

"Ethel Winter, the girl in red who appeared in this number, is an absolute dream of a dancer."

By Winifred Bissinger, The Daily Mirror, Nov.15, 1955.

Graham Recreates Clytemnestra: "Miss Graham, on stage throughout, performs her difficult steps with amazing inner strength and agility. Her attractive group is excellent. It would be hard to find better modern dance support that in Yuriko as Iphigenia, Ethel Winter as Helen of Troy, and Helen McGehee as Electra."

By Frances Herridge, New York Post, 1958.

"...there were top rank performances by the beautiful Ethel Winter (who is dancing magnificently this season) as Joan."
By Walter Terry, N.Y Herald Tribune., 1958.

"Ethel Winter was the principal female figure who raced across the stage as if borne by the wind or paused in lovely balance mid-stage as if reclining on an unseen breeze."

By Walter Terry, N.Y. Herald Tribune, April 18, 1961.

"Ethel Winter, emerging as Aphrodite from a heart-shaped enclosure by Isamu Noguchi, is jaunty and heartless and immensely fascinating."

By Frances Herridge, New York Post, March 5, 1958.

"Ethel Winter makes Aphrodite permeating vulgar and vicious (Though half an hour earlier she was the beautiful and heartbreaking Joan of Arc in "Seraphic Dialogue.")

By John Martin, New York Times, March 11, 1962.

"Ethel Winter is magnificently repulsive as Aphrodite. Her every movement is pert, defiant, malicious or obscene. We ask ourselves: Can this be the exquisite Saint Joan of Seraphic Dialogue? A more dazzling exhibition of dramatic virtuosity has never been seen."

The Martha Graham Season, Broadway Theatre, March 4-18, 1962.

"Ethel Winter was my own favorite, for she possesses a gaiety and bold charm which lights up her personality."

Dancing Times, Oct., 1963.

"It was performed with dramatic power, emotional sensitivity and a spiritual glow by Ethel Winter as the total image of Joan and Yuriko as Joan the Maid."

By Walter Terry, New York Herald Tribune, 1964.

"She has bequeathed her own role of the Bride in "Appalachian Spring" to Ethel Winter, and last night Miss Winter gave a radiant performance of the girl-bride-woman who faced a frontier with fear, a touch of loneliness but also with faith and fetching gaiety.
Miss Winter was also superb as the figute in red – sometimes as immobile as a statue and again as propulsive as a flaming rocket – in that glorious Graham work about playfulness and love and youth, "Diversion of Angels".

By Walter Terry, N.Y. Herald Tribune

"In "Frontier", an American perspective of the plains, we found Ethel Winter recreating the part Miss Graham once danced. No one else could have done greater justice to this solo tha Miss Winter. In its simplicity, changing from carefree lightness to determination and strength, it still fulfills its task of bringing back to our mind the spikrit of the pioneer days. Miss Winter gave it color and dimension."

By Walter Sorell, Dance Observer, 1964.

"As for the historic solo, "Frontier", it remains a monument of towering proportions in the filed of American dance. No one who saw Miss Graham dance it will ever forget the experience. Her successor in the part, Ethel Winter, quiet rightly interprets the dance in her own way and in that way, she too is triumphant. She communicates in movement and in pose sweetness and strength, daring and seriousness, gaiety and indomitable hope. This solo is the striking statement of the American pioneer spirit and we should pray that Miss Graham never permits it to leave her active repertory again."
By Walter Terry, New York Herald Tribune, August 17, 1964.

It is a pleasure, however, to view the haunting, lyrical "Appalachian Spring" again, and to see Ethel Winter dance with astonishing brilliance the role Graham used to dance. In a season of forlorn, tawdry fare, Miss Graham has given us dazzling distinction."
CUE, November 13, 1965.

"The quality of "Appalachian Spring" is that of a young America growing, when everything was a virgin. As the bride, Ethel Winter danced with a sharp, alert brightness, darting happily inside the choreography, and missing perhaps only the serene confidence that Miss Graham herself once brought to the role."
By Clive Barnes, The New York Times, November 8, 1965.

"Against this background Ethel Winter in Miss Graham's original role of the bride danced with a thoroughly expressive virtuosity, unbroken grace, and the needed intensity as an actress. She is complimented by Robert Cohan's expressiveness, both in tensely dramatic movement and in a cheerful agility that surprises the viewer repeatedly."
By Bill Fanning, The Catholic News, November 18, 1965.

"Secular Games," playful and beautiful and bursting with glorious designs in space –some of the fights of the men dancers were breathtaking –was followed by the radiance of "Appalachian Spring," a Graham masterwork in which the role of the Bride is now danced by Ethel Winter. Miss Winter does not imitate her illustrious predecessor – who could copy a Graham? –but she probes the role deeply and delivers it in her own sweet and glowing terms."
By Walter Terry, New York Herald Tribune, November 3, 1965.

"The masterpiece "Appalachian Spring." with Ethel Winter in the role made famous by Miss graham herself, was as magnificent a theater work as ever. Miss Winter, darting and supple, did excellently."

By Clive Barnes, The New York Times, November 3, 1965.

"Restoration inevitably meant abdication of roles that had been for Martha Graham highly personal experiences. This season marks Miss Graham's formal bequeathing of these history-making roles to her younger dancers. "I trust Ethel (Winter), Helen (McGehee) and Yuriko implicitly," she said. She had to, because she was so busy with new works, the costumes, the lights and almost everything else that surrounds the working of their company that she had no time even to see "Appalachin Spring" before the opening night.

This glowing, passionate work, set to Aaron Copland's lucidly pastoral score, proved everything that memory promised, the very best Graham. And Ethel Winter, one of the very best Graham-trained dancers, danced with a grace and joy of both body and spirit. That all three works will live is important. They are Miss Graham's immortality. But, when she was asked about plans for more revivals, she was not worried about immortality. She simply answered: "I do not have time to make plans."

Newsweek, November 15, 1965.

"Ethel Winter, as Joan at the moment of her apotheosis, is one of the best dancers in the company, deeply feminine, with a sense of humor and patrician beauty and a wide, acute, and powerful range of movement."

By Kathleen Cannell, The Christian Science Monitor, December 2, 1966.

"This is "Night Journey," Martha Graham's celebrated dance-drama of the Oedipus myth. The role of Jocasta is, perhaps, more closely identified with Miss Graham, the dancer, than any other role in her remarkable repertory. Yet last night, at the Mark Hellinger Theater, she did not dance it. Along with other characterizations she has made famous, she has turned Jocasta over to a younger artist, in this case, to the beautiful and enormously talented Ethel Winter.

Miss Winter, who now dances the Bride (created by Graham herself) in "Appalachian Spring," is superb in her inherited part. In "Night Journey," however, she is merely on the threshold of discovering who Jocasta is.

Yes, she communicated tragedy, but not the enormity of crime committed, such as Miss Graham herself projected. Yes, she stretches a leg ear-high, but one does not hear the mute cry from the loins which Graham made you hear. Yes, she slides to the floor in a great gesture of despair, but it is non monumental self-abasement. Miss Winter, of course, is quite right in not attempting to copy the blazing, volcanic Graham. She didn't copy her in either "Salem Shore" or "Appalachian Spring" and in "Spring" she has a winner on her own merits. With "Night Journey," she will do the same, but it may take a little time. I'm a long-time admirer of Miss Winter and her high dance art, and I think I can predict that she will find her own way to Jocasta's tormented heart."

By Walter Terry, World Journal Tribune, New York, March 1, 1967.

"Last night the task of following fell to Ethel Winter, dancing Jocasta for the first time. It was, very properly, a performance almost totally different from Miss Graham's own prototype. Now and again one could detect a striking similarity, an arrowshot of likeness that sent my mind back 12 years or more when I saw Miss Graham's Jocasta. But such similarities are almost by chance –Miss Winter, naturally, goes her own way.

Miss Winter is full of blood, full of life. This is almost as much like Shakespeare's Gertrude as Sophocles's Joscasts, yet no matter. Her warmth is a far cry from the black-cold sense of destiny suggested by Miss Graham herself in the role, yet hardly less effective. Indeed in its natural pathos –this is such a human and cuddly Jocasta –there are even occasion gains her, and when this girl-mother faces the truth she faces with dignity rather than grandeur. This is possibly what we need in our day and age –a Jocasta to submerge with an abstracted yet decent gesture of human impotence, rather than a proudly tragic furl of heroic satiation. Miss Winter, feminine and frustrated, is a Jocasta for our times."

By Clive Barnes, The New York Times, March 1, 1967.

"Appalachian Spring," with its great Aaron Copland score, has been a Graham staple for more than 20 years. Ethel Winter now danced the Bride, and, on Saturday, she gave a performance of such inner radiance, such outward beauty of step and stance that it was impossible not to cry. I have seen "Spring" many, many times, but I find something new every time amid its inexhaustible choreographic riches."

By Walter Terry, N.Y. Herald Tribune, 1967.

"Ethel Winter has another kind of task in "Appalachian Spring." She must bring to life the pioneer bride, who gazes out on the plains where she will find her future world and accepts with joy the harshness of the wilderness because her man will be at her side. All the dancer's natural, warm, womanly loveliness is in her performance.

Miss Winter faced her greatest test later in the season when she danced Jocasta in "Night Journey" for the first time. So utterly do we live Jocasta's agony in this work –no matter how often we see it –that the moment when Oedipus blinds himself and then withdraws in self banishment comes with a shock of surprise. Where Miss Graham gave to Jocasta the universality, the larger-than-life quality that the Greek dramatists and Shakespeare commanded, Miss Winter draws the picture of a very human woman, stunned and shattered by her appalling life. There is glorious dancing here. And over and over again a pose, the outline of a body, gives us the very essence of Graham. But Miss Winter's Jocasta is her very own, and within the framework of that supremely noble work it is a very satisfying one."

By P.W. Manchester, Christian Sc. Monitor

"It was Miss Winter (I once called her the "Winter of our content," and I'm too thrifty to use the quip only once) who starred in "Appalachian Spring," dancing the role created, of course, by Miss Graham herself. Set to Aaron Copland's sophisticated homespun music, "Appalachian Spring" has a kind of frontier sparseness to it, suggesting a world of hope, space and plenty.

This is one of the great Graham works, and it was a special pleasure last season when it was revived with Miss Winter inheriting Miss Graham's own role as the frontier Bride. Then Miss Winter danced it with a deliquescent sweetness, yet even in so doing, missed some element of Spartan pioneering that was always inherent in Miss Graham's own treatment of the part.

Now Miss Winter seems to have learned her lesson, and while the Bride is made as fresh and as young as ever, she gives the role a new quality of hardness, a hint of endurance beneath the bridal floss. "

By Clive Barnes, New York Times, February 1967.

"She has bequeathed her own role of the Bride in "Appalachian Spring" to Ethel Winter, and last night Miss Winter gave a radiant performance of the girl-bride-woman who faced a frontier with fear, a touch of loneliness but also with faith and fetching gaiety.

Miss Winter was also superb as the figure in red –sometimes as immobile as a statue and again as propulsive as a flaming rocket –in that glorious Graham work about playfulness and love and youth, "Diversion of Angels".

By Walter Terry, N.Y. Herald Tribune, 1967.

Roles performed by Ethel Winter with the Martha Graham Company

Choreography	Year of Premiere	Year and Roles Performed by Ethel Winter
Primitive Mystery	1931	1948 Group
Frontier	1935	1964 Solo, 1st to succeed Martha Graham
Every Soul is a Circus	1939	1944 Group, 1st role with the Graham Company
El Penitente	1940	1948 Main Role, succeeded Martha Graham
Letter to the World	1940	1946 Group, the Fairie Queen, succeeded Nina Fonaroff1950 Young Love, succeeded Pearl Lang
Punch and Judy	1941	1948 Pretty Polly, succeeded Pearl Lang 1950 Little Girl, succeeded Nina Fonaroff
Salem Shore	1943	1947 Solo, 1st to succeed Martha Graham
Death and Entrances	1943	1946 One of the young girls, succeeded Pearl Lang 1958 A sister, succeeded Pearl Lang
Herodiade	1944	1963, solo, 1st to succeed Martha Graham
Appalachian Spring	1944	1946 Group 1965 The Bride, 1st to succeed Martha Graham

Choreography	Year of Premiere	Year and Roles Performed by Ethel Winter
Dark Meadow	1946	1946 Group
Night Journey	1947	1947 Group1963 Jocasta, 1st to succeed Martha Graham
Diversions of Angels	1948	1950 Group1955 The Girl in Red, succeeded Pearl Lang
Ardent Song	1954	1955 Dawn, succeeded Pearl Lang
Seraphic Dialog	1955	1955 Joan as the Maid, succeeded Patricia Birch1959 Main Joan, shared with Linda Hodes
Clytemnestra	1958	1958, Helen of Troy, created on her
Episodes	1959	1959 Group
Acrobats of God	1960	1960 Group
Alcestis	1960	1960 Group
One More Gaudy Night	1961	1961 Cleopatra, created on her
Phaedre	1962	1962 Aphrodite, created on her
Part Real Part Dream	1965	1965 succeeded Matt Turney
Coretege of Eagles	1967	1967 The Andramache, last piece created on Ethel Winter

Ethel Winter Dance Company

The Ethel Winter Dance Company, based in New York City, was founded in 1962 and continued to perform until 1969. The company consisted of dancers mainly from the Martha Graham School who later went on to perform with Martha Graham, Paul Taylor, Sophie Maslow, Glen Tetly among others. Over the years Company members included: Moss Cohen, Richard Kuch, Lynne Kothera, Stanley Berke, Wesley Fata, Molly Moore, Linda Shoop, Jaunita Londono, Noemi Lapzeson, Kazuko Hirabayashi, Marilyn Liebman, William Dugan, Eileen Cropley, Sheila Komer and on certain occasions, University dance students joined in group pieces. Costumes were designed by Ethel Winter and sets designed by Charles Hyman. Music collaborators include Joseph Liebling, Eugene Lester, Arthur Murphy and Gwen Watson.

Appearances of the Ethel Winter Dance Company

Slippery Rock State Teachers College, Slippery Rock, Pennsylvania

Brockport College, Rochester, New York

Jewish Community Center, Atlantic City, New Jersey

St. Mary's College, Baltimore, Maryland

University of the South, Sewanse, Tennessee

Adelphi University, Garden City, Long Island

Teachers College - Columbia University, New York City

Boone Institute, Boone, North Carolina

Bridgewater College, Bridgewater, Virginia

Waynesboro Concert Association, Waynesboro, Virginia

Wisconsin State College, Stevens Point, Wisconsin

Lakeland College, Sheboygan, Wisconsin

Civic Music Association, Dixon, Illinois

St. Lawrence University, Canton, New York

West Virginia State College, Institute, West Virginia

Y.M.H. A. (Young Men's Hebrew Association) New York City

University of Rhode Island, Kingston, Road Island

Bloomsberg State College, Bloomsberg, Pennsylvania

Keuka Park State Teachers College, Keuka Park, New Xork

Wisconsin State Teachers College, Whitewater, Wisconsin

Lindenwood College, St. Charles Missouri

Mt. Aloysius Junior College, Cresson, Pennsylvania

East Tennessee State University, Johnson City, Tennessee

State University Agricultural Institute, Canton, New York

Wheaton College, Norton, Massachusetts

Modern Dance Educational Foundation, Teaneck, New Jersey

Choreographies by Ethel Winter

1944   *En Dolor* (Solo)

Music: Manuel de Falla

En Dolor has been described as "a lament of memory." The piece portrays a woman mourning a personal loss and she must deal with her grief and anger.

1946   *In the Clearing* (Solo)

Original Music: Gregory Tucker

1946   *Heartbreak* (solo)

Original Music: Betty Jean Walburg

1961   *Night Forest* (group)

Original Music: Eugene Lester

Set Design: Charles Hyman (2 groupings of Poles)

Night Forest was based on primitive dance form, linking life and death, good and evil with animistic worship. The piece is a play within a play. The Night Creature in this dance symbolizes fear, specifically fear of death. The dance unfolds in 3 sections: Parade, The Play (Night Creature, Haunted Maiden, Chorus) and Celebration.

1961   *Fun and Fancy* (group)

Music: Paul Bowles

A joyful frolic, utilizing the satiric qualities of the music. Also described as a humorous and breezy choreography of music and movement.

1961   *Magic Mirror* (group)

Original Music: Arthur Murphy

Set Design: Charles Hyman (a revolving mirror)

This work has been described as a modern fairy tale. "A fantasy of ourselves". In fantasy, a young girl, dreams of her Prince to come. He awakens her to love. The dream experience appears as a reality. When she loses her Prince all becomes a nightmare. The spectres enter to torment the girl in her loneliness. Characters include a girl, a boy, and the spectres.

1961   *Suite of Three* (Solo)

Original Music: Joseph Liebling

Suite of Three is a dance of three moods: Anticipation, Disillusion and Exaltation.

1965   *Poems* (later called *Two Shadows Passed* with original music: Gwen Watson)

Music: Paul Hindemith

Set Design: Charles Hyman

Poems is an interpretation based on the Poetry of Paul Verlaine and is portrayed in 6 sections: Through old unpeopled gardens, Tears fall in my heart, The sky will be all blue, My course is blind, Let's dance a jig, The last rays of the setting sun.

1965   *Tempi Variations* (group)

Music: J.S.Bach

Sections: Andante, Allegro, Lento, Presto, Mysterioso, Furioso, and Finale

1969   *Won and Lost* (solo), later called *Night Conversations*

Original Music: Gwen Watson

1969   *The Beloit Festival*

Barbara Allen: Folk Ballad (solo)

Aquarius, Diamonds are a girls best friend,

Watching all the girls go by (groups for entire affiliate artists)

These pieces were unique in that they were choreographed for the entire group of Affiliate Artists Group including musicians, artists, and dancers, for the Beloit Festival in 1969.

1970　*An Age of Innocence* (trio)

Music: Scott Joplin

A parody on The Victim, The Villain, The Hero (a Dudley Doowright take off)

1971　*Descent to Earthly Delights* (Group)

Original Music: Harry Partch

Set Design: Charles Hyman)

Descent to Earthly Delights is a celebration of being on Earth. The music composition was unique in that the composer made his own instruments.

(1970)　*Spiritual Passage* (solo)

Music: J.S.Bach, Prelude from Well Tempered Clavier

A lyrical piece that is a journey of sorts...

This choreography is currently being revived by Ethel Winter.

Additional repertoire perfrmed by the Ethel Winter Dance Company

1962　*Songbag* (group)

Choreography: Sophie Maslow

Music: Traditional

Songbag is a lively arrangement of Southern and Appalachian Mountain folk-tunes.

Chronology

1924 Ethel Winter, born in Wrentham, Massachusetts on June 18

1941 Attends Bennington College in Vermont to pursue a degree in the Theater Arts Department, Dance Department Chair, Martha Hill

1943 Worked with Sophie Maslow for the first time at Bennington College learned Maslow's choreography Sarabande

1944 Choreographed *En Dolor* as a student at Bennington, age 19

1945 First performance with the Graham Company at Bennington College Danced a chorus role in *Every Soul is a Circus* as a junior student

1945 Went to NY for the Winter Season and joined the Graham Company on tour for six weeks as a senior student. Graduated from Bennington College with a BA degree in Theater Arts

1946 Danced in the original cast of *Dark Meadows*. Performs in *Death and Entrances, Letter to the World, Appalachian Spring, Every Soul is a Circus*

1946 Chosen to perform her solos *En Dolor, In the Clearing* and *Heartbreak* at the Young Men's Hebrew Association in New York City

1947 Danced in the original cast of *Night Journey*

1948 Toured with Erick Hawkins and Stuart Hodes in Theater Dance Pieces Performed Graham's Salem Shore and El Penitente. Salem Shore was the first role Graham relinquished to Ethel Winter

1949	Became ill and takes 1 year off from the Graham Company Returns to Bennington College to teach while working on her Masters Degree
1950	Marries Charles Hyman, faculty member in the Theater Arts Department at Bennington Returns to the Graham Company for the European Tour
1951	Graduates from Bennington College with a Masters Degree in Dance
1952	Performances with City Center Opera Co., choreography by Sophie Maslow and Charles Weidman
1954	Performs in Broadway show *Ankles Away*, choreography by Tony Charmoli
1954	Danced in the original cast of Sokolow's *Lyric Suite*
1955-1956	Rejoins Graham Company for the Asian Tour
1957	*Summer stock in Brandywine, Pennsylvania*, choreography Nelle Fisher. Danced in Graham film A Dancer's World
1958	Danced in Graham film *Appalachian Spring*. Danced role of Helen of Troy, created for her, in Graham's Clytemnestyra Son David Hyman is born
1959	Danced in original cast of *Episodes*
1960	Danced in original cast of Graham's *Acrobats of God and Alcestis*
1961	Danced role of Cleopatra, created for her in Graham's *One More Gaudy Night*
1962-1969	Founded The Ethel Winter Dance Company. Tours throughout the United States with her company for 7 years
1962	Danced Aphrodite in *Phaedra*, her first villainous role specifically created for Ethel Winter

1963	First dancer to revive and perform Graham's role in *Herodiade* Ethel Winter, Mary Hinkson and Bert Ross invited to London as pioneers in the Graham Technique
1964	Invited to Israel as a founding member of the Betshava Dance Company and sets her work *Fun and Fancy* on the Company First dancer to revive and perform Graham's role in *Frontier*
1964-1970	Performed each year in New York City Hanukkah Festival as guest artist Sophie Maslow choreographer. Guest performances with Maslow Company and praised for role of Leah in *Dybbuk*.
1965	Choreographed and danced in *La Traviata* for City Center Opera Co. Took over Martha's role as the bride in *Appalachian Spring*
1967	Danced the role of Andromache in *Cortege of Eagles*, the last role Graham created on Ethel Winter
1967	Becomes the first dancer to be chosen for the Affiliate Artist Program Residency was at Hood College which included teaching, lectures and performances First dancer to take over Graham's role of Jocasta in *Night Journey*
1968	In Hershey, Pennsylvania, she performed Jane Dudley's *HarmonicaBreakdown* TV Summer teaching, choreography and performance at Long Beach, California
1969	After over 20 years: Ethel Winter leaves the Graham Company, continues teaching at the Graham School
1969	Appointed Affiliate Artist at Point Park College in Pittsburgh Guest of Pittsburg Ballet Company, performs own choreographies: Suite of Three, En Dolor and Spiritual Passage

Festival in Wisconsin, choreographs *Barbara Allen Ballad* and the finale *Aquarius* from Hair for the entire company of the Affiliate Artist Program

1970   Guest artist for Salt Lake City's Dance Repertory Theater

1971   Choreographed dance filmed for the Mr. Roger's Neighborhood show Summer teaching and choreographing at University of Hawaii

1972   Summer teaching, choreographing and performing at Long Beach, California

1973-   Director of Graham School
1974

1975   Guest artist for Santa Fe Dance Theater, staged choreography of *Fun and Fancy*

1980's Guest teaching in England, Ilkley, Leeds, Bradford (1983), Darlington (1984), Newcastle (1985)

1988   First summer teaching in Bern, Switzerland

1997   Assistant to Sophie Maslow at Saratoga Springs, New York

1998   Assistant to Sophie Maslow for the revival of The Village I knew

1999   Guest teaching at Southern Methodist University and Miami School of the Arts

2001   Summer teaching at Frostbury University, Maryland

2003   Departure from Julliard School after 50 years, continues to guest teach and her association with Martha Graham School for Contemporary Dance

Appendix data collected by Kathryn Eggert in collaboration with Ethel Winter and Charles Hyman.

Literature on Martha Graham

de Mille, Agnes: Martha: The Life and Work of Martha Graham, 1991

Helpern, Alice: The Technique of Martha Graham, Margan Press, New York, 1994

Morgan, Barbara: Martha Graham – Sixteen Dances in Photographs, Morgan & Morgan, Inc., New York, 1980

Mitchell, Jack: American Dance Portfolio, Dodd, Mead & Company, New York, 1964

Stodelle, Ernestine: Deep Song, Dance Story of Martha Graham, 1984

Tracy, Robert, ed.: Goddess, Martha Graham dancers remember, 1996

Printed in the United Kingdom
by Lightning Source UK Ltd.
124919UK00001B/448-450/A

9 783833 463273